Grandma Low's Pick of

4-Words
of Wisdom

by Julia Hsu Low

Grandma Low's Pick of **4-Words of Wisdom**

Illustrations copyright by their respective artists:

Aleks Banner
All category title drawings except chapter 1; 1.7, 1.8; 4.6; 5.1; chapter 7; 9.9; 11.7; chapter 13; 15.2, 15.3, 15.9; chapter 20; chapter 23; 24.2; 26.4, 26.6, 26.7; 28.9; chapter 29; chapter 30; chapter 31; chapter 32 except 32.7; 33.6; chapter 34; 35.5; chapter 36 except 36.2; chapter 37; 38.2, 38.3.

Erica Femino
1.2; 2.1, 2.4, 2.7, 2.8, 2.9; chapter 3; 4.2; 6.1; chapter 8; chapter 9 except 9.9; chapter 12 except 12.1, 12.5, 12.6, 12.8; chapter 14; 16.1, 16.5, 16.6; chapter 17 except 17.2; chapter 19 except 19.2 & 19.4; chapter 25; chapter 27; chapter 28 except 28.9; 32.7; 33.1, 33.2, 33.7, 33.9, 33.10, 33.11, 33.12; chapter 35 except 35.5; chapter 38 except 38.2 & 38.3.

Suzanna Yang Hsu
2.2, 2.3, 2.5, 2.6; 5.3, 5.4, 5.5; 12.1, 12.5, 12.6, 12.8; 19.2, 19.4.

Stacey Westley Low
6.3; 12.10 (shared with Erica); 17.2; 33.3, 33.4, 33.5, 33.8; 36.2.

Samantha Pickett
Category title drawing for chapter 1; chapter 1 except 1.2, 1.7, 1.8; 4.1, 4.3, 4.4, 4.5; 5.2, 5.6; 6.2, 6.4, 6.5, 6.6; chapter 10; chapter 11 except 11.7; chapter 15 except 15.2, 15.3, 15.9; 16.2, 16.3; chapter 18; chapter 21; chapter 22; chapter 24 except 24.2; chapter 26 except 26.4, 26.6, 26.7.

Sophia Xu
16.4.

*

Graphic design by Aleks Banner   www.aleksbanner.com

Printed in Somerville, MA, USA, by Gangi Printing. www.gangiprinting.com

ISBN 978-0-9855338-0-9

www.grandmalow.com

画	畫	huà	pictures
语	語	yǔ	words
并	并	bìng	side by side
茂	茂	mào	to complement, splendid

A picture is a gateway to pleasure and knowledge.

A charm all its own.

INTRODUCTION

One summer day in July, 2011, while waiting at a traffic light on Memorial Drive along the Charles River towards Boston, Massachusetts, I noticed the car in front of me with a New Hampshire license plate bearing the state motto:

"Live Free or Die."

不自由，毋宁死

不自由，毋寧死

Just four little words, I thought, carry such a profound and powerful message. My mind immediately was flooded with all the frequently used 4-word Chinese idioms and expressions I learned as a child growing up in Shanghai, China. Over the next few days, I began to collect idioms and expressions from family members and friends. Thus began my project.

Like idioms of other languages, they often contain hidden messages mostly related to life and living. Among the three, four, five, six and 7-word Chinese idioms, the most popular are the 4-word ones. They are time and space saving and economical as they offer the most concise use of words. Chinese idioms can be traced back to ancient dynasties, often quoted in classical literature, poetry and historical legends. It is estimated there are more than 30,000 Chinese idioms.

A few selected idioms in this book reflect the period of feudalistic society in China when a gender gap existed, and women played a less important role (see 25.1, 25.6, 25.8 and 29.6). In an effort to adapt to modern times, the expressions have been carefully worded to portray a more contemporary view.

Expressions, however, differ from region to region and they change with time as new trends are introduced. In recent years, we often find 4-word descriptions and expressions on restaurant menus, eye-catching advertising titles and newspaper headlines. Speakers and writers often borrow specific lines to connect with the audience and readers.

The purpose of this book is to bring fun and humor to readers learning the Chinese language as well as Chinese-speaking readers learning matching idioms and expressions in English. It is not designed to be a text book.

Sir Francis Bacon once said, "Knowledge is power."
I hope readers will find this book educational, entertaining, informative and interesting, and I wish you all fulfill your reading pleasure.

Julia Hsu Low
Watertown, Massachusetts
2012

FEATURES

The unique format of this book is designed to provide easy reading for all readers - English-speaking and non-English speaking alike.

Chinese characters: While the traditional Chinese characters (fanti) evolved from pictorial symbols, simplified Chinese characters (jianti) will be used as the primary choice, accompanied by fanti along side. Please see the example on the opposite page:

Drawings accompany each idiom to help enhance visual memory. Each artist represented here has his or her own creative style, to help deliver the message of the specific idiom or expression. We ask readers to also participate in using his or her own imagination to help understand the message.

Lines in italics indicate frequently used expressions in English, quotes or writer's comments.

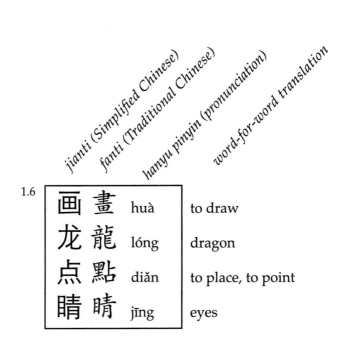

jianti (Simplified Chinese)
fanti (Traditional Chinese)
hanyu pinyin (pronunciation)
word-for-word translation

1.6

画	畫	huà	to draw
龙	龍	lóng	dragon
点	點	diǎn	to place, to point
睛	睛	jīng	eyes

The life of a dragon is in its eyes.

Concentrate on the focal point of any task.

Cherry on the sundae.
Crowning touch.

CONTENTS

内容　内容

Grandma Low's Pick of

4 - Words

of Wisdom

ANIMAL INSPIRED

1

动物型

動物型

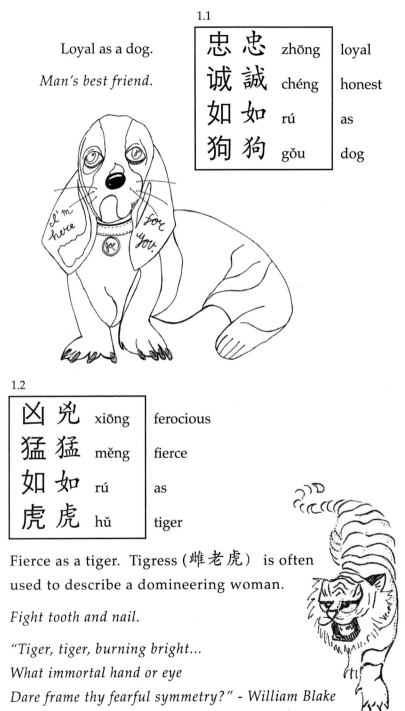

1.1

Loyal as a dog.

Man's best friend.

忠	忠	zhōng	loyal
诚	誠	chéng	honest
如	如	rú	as
狗	狗	gǒu	dog

1.2

凶	兇	xiōng	ferocious
猛	猛	měng	fierce
如	如	rú	as
虎	虎	hǔ	tiger

Fierce as a tiger. Tigress (雌老虎) is often used to describe a domineering woman.

Fight tooth and nail.

"Tiger, tiger, burning bright...
What immortal hand or eye
Dare frame thy fearful symmetry?" - William Blake

1.3

画	畫	huà	to draw
蛇	蛇	shé	snake
添	添	tiān	to add
足	足	zú	feet

Unnecessary action may cause negative effect.

Quit while you are ahead.

Don't waste your time.

*Don't cast your
pearls before swine.*

1.4

对	對	duì	to face
牛	牛	niú	cow
弹	彈	tán	to play
琴	琴	qín	musical instrument

1.5

懒	懶	lǎn	lazy
惰	惰	duò	idle
如	如	rú	as
猪	豬	zhū	pig

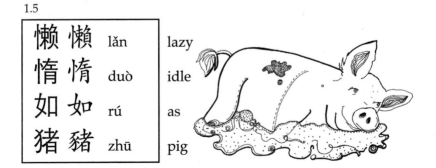

Lazy as a pig.

Lazy bones. Lazy as a sloth.

The life of a dragon is in its eyes.

Concentrate on the focal point of any task.

1.6

Cherry on the sundae.

Crowning touch.

画	畫	huà	to draw
龙	龍	lóng	dragon
点	點	diǎn	to place, to point
睛	睛	jīng	eyes

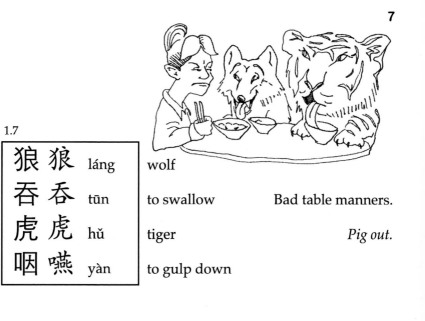

1.7

狼	狼	láng	wolf
吞	吞	tūn	to swallow
虎	虎	hǔ	tiger
咽	嚥	yàn	to gulp down

Bad table manners.

Pig out.

1.8

走	走	zǒu	to ride, to walk
马	馬	mǎ	horse
观	觀	guān	to view
花	花	huā	flowers

Not paying attention to details.

Superficial knowledge about surroundings.

Sunday drive.

1.9

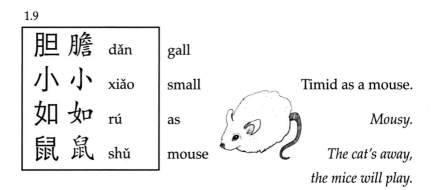

胆	膽	dǎn	gall
小	小	xiǎo	small
如	如	rú	as
鼠	鼠	shǔ	mouse

Timid as a mouse.

Mousy.

The cat's away,
the mice will play.

APPEARANCE

外貌

外貌

2.1

五	五	wǔ	five
官	官	guān	sense organs
端	端	duān	proper
正	正	zhèng	straight

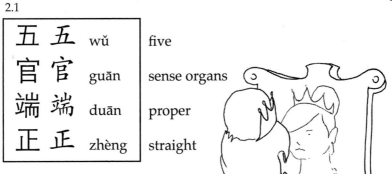

Good features.

Picture perfect.

2.2

珠	珠	zhū	pearl
光	光	guāng	glitter
宝	寶	bǎo	precious*
气	氣	qì	air

Jewelry covered woman looks unattractive* (antonym).

"Gild the lily." - William Shakespeare

2.3

一	一	yì	one
丝	絲	sī	silk thread
不	不	bú	not
挂	掛	guà	to hang

Naked. *Birthday suit.*

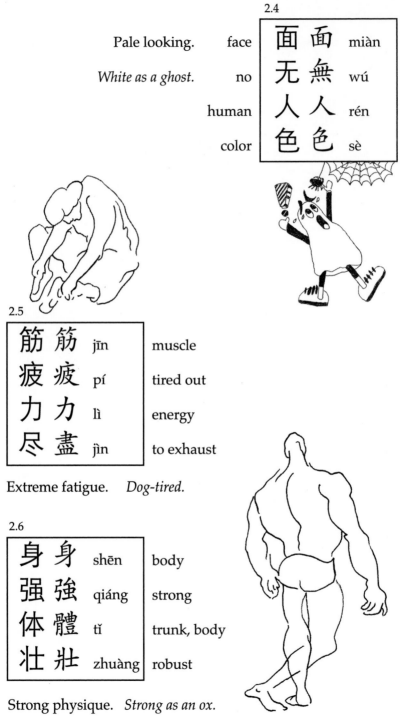

2.4

Pale looking.	face	面	面	miàn
White as a ghost.	no	无	無	wú
	human	人	人	rén
	color	色	色	sè

2.5

筋	筋	jīn	muscle
疲	疲	pí	tired out
力	力	lì	energy
尽	盡	jìn	to exhaust

Extreme fatigue.   *Dog-tired.*

2.6

身	身	shēn	body
强	強	qiáng	strong
体	體	tǐ	trunk, body
壮	壯	zhuàng	robust

Strong physique.   *Strong as an ox.*

2.7

满	滿	mǎn	full
面	面	miàn	face
春	春	chūn	spring
风	風	fēng	breeze

Jovial appearance.

Mr. and Mrs. Sunshine.

2.8

衣	衣	yī	clothes
冠	冠	guān	head gear
不	不	bù	not
整	整	zhěng	neat, tidy

Sloppy appearance. *Slob.*

2.9

坐	坐	zuò	to sit
立	立	lì	to stand
不	不	bù	not
安	安	ān	calm, stable

Nervous.   *Nervous Nellie.*

ATTITUDE

3

态度
態度

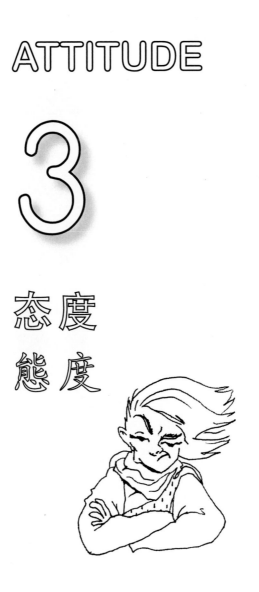

3.1

积	積	jī	to store up
极	極	jí	extreme
乐	樂	lè	happy
观	觀	guān	outlook

Positive outlook on life.

Happy-go-lucky.

3.2

自	自	zì	self
得	得	dé	to acquire
其	其	qí	that of
乐	樂	lè	happiness

To be content.

"What, me worry?" - Alfred E. Neuman

14

3.3

愁	愁	chóu	worrisome
眉	眉	méi	eyebrows
苦	苦	kǔ	hardship, sad
脸	臉	liǎn	face

Sad. Anxious.

Worrywart.

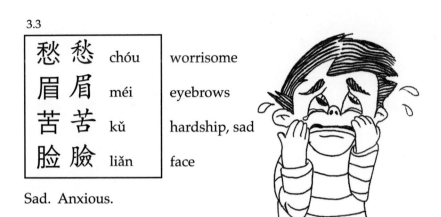

3.4

置	置	zhì	to set aside
之	之	zhī	something
不	不	bù	no
理	理	lǐ	attention, action

Doesn't care. Unconcerned.

Don't give a damn. Fall on deaf ears.

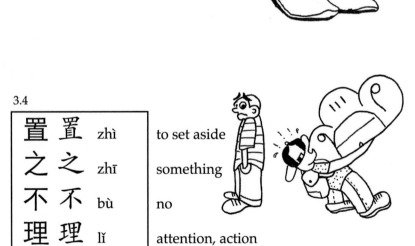

3.5

泰	泰	tài	peaceful
然	然	rán	like that, then
自	自	zì	self
若	若	ruò	as such

Relaxed.

Carefree. Easy come, easy go.

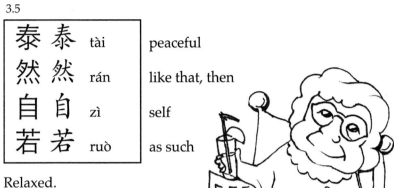

3.6

心	心	xīn	heart
不	不	bú	not
在	在	zài	at
焉	焉	yān	where, how

Not focused. Absent-minded.

Scatterbrain. Head in the clouds.

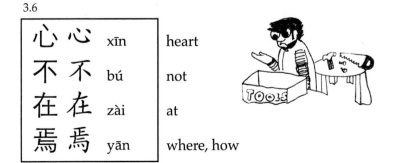

BEHAVIOR

行为

行為

4.1

安	安	ān	to secure
分	分	fèn	one's share
守	守	shǒu	to guard
己	己	jǐ	self

Proper behavior.   *"Know your place." - William Safire*

4.2

有	有	yǒu	to have
始	始	shǐ	beginning
无	無	wú	to have no
终	終	zhōng	ending

Lack of follow through.

Gives up easily.

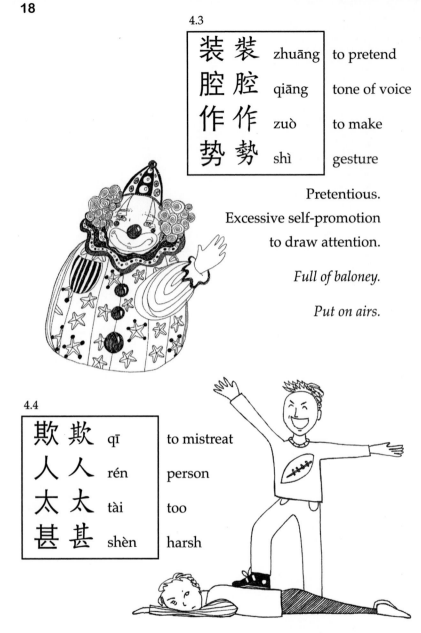

4.3

裝	裝	zhuāng	to pretend
腔	腔	qiāng	tone of voice
作	作	zuò	to make
勢	勢	shì	gesture

Pretentious.
Excessive self-promotion
to draw attention.

Full of baloney.

Put on airs.

4.4

欺	欺	qī	to mistreat
人	人	rén	person
太	太	tài	too
甚	甚	shèn	harsh

Bullying.

Big bully.

4.5

奉	奉	fèng	to respect
公	公	gōng	justice
守	守	shǒu	to abide
法	法	fǎ	law

Follow the law.

Law abiding.

Straight and narrow.

4.6

自	自	zì	self
高	高	gāo	tall
自	自	zì	self
大	大	dà	big

Conceited.　Vain.

Full of yourself.

BEAUTY

5

美观

美觀

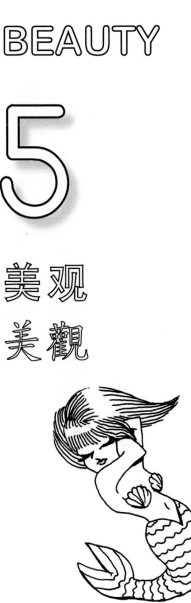

5.1

十	十	shí	ten
全	全	quán	complete
十	十	shí	ten
美	美	měi	beautiful

Ten out of ten.
May apply to objects
or tasks.

Perfect ten.

5.2

美	美	měi	beauty
中	中	zhōng	among
不	不	bù	no, not
足	足	zú	enough, sufficient

Imperfect. May apply to objects or tasks.

Something's missing. A fly in the ointment.

5.3

美	美	měi	beautiful
如	如	rú	as
天	天	tiān	heaven
仙	仙	xiān	angel

As beautiful as an angel from heaven.

Angelic.   *Angel face.*

5.4

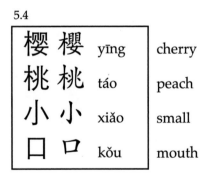

樱	櫻	yīng	cherry
桃	桃	táo	peach
小	小	xiǎo	small
口	口	kǒu	mouth

Cherry-shaped lips.

Pretty as a peach.

Indulged. Spoiled.

Daddy's little girl. Apple of my eye.

5.5

娇	嬌	jiāo	spoiled, pampered
小	小	xiǎo	petite, cute
玲	玲	líng	clever
珑	瓏	lóng	lively

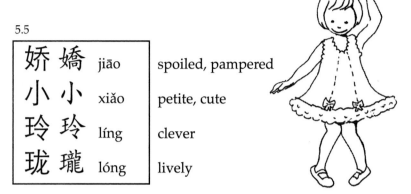

5.6

眉	眉	méi	eyebrows
清	清	qīng	clear, bright
目	目	mù	eyes
秀	秀	xiù	beautiful

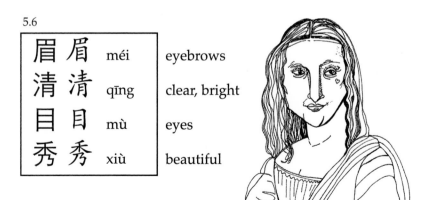

Natural beauty.

Natural good looks.

BUSINESS

6

事业
事業

6.1

开	開	kāi	to open
门	門	mén	door
大	大	dà	big
吉	吉	jí	luck

Grand opening!

Good luck!

6.2

大	大	dà	big
功	功	gōng	achievement
告	告	gào	to announce
成	成	chéng	to complete

A job well done.   *Mission accomplished.*

6.3

股	股	gǔ	stocks, shares
市	市	shì	market
下	下	xià	downward
降	降	jiàng	to fall

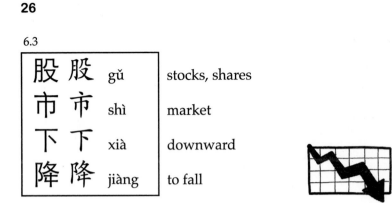

Stock market has fallen!

Bear market. "What goes up must come down." - Isaac Newton

6.4

动	動	dòng	to motion
机	機	jī	opportunity
不	不	bù	no, not
良	良	liáng	good, fine

Unethical motive. Scamming.

If you believe that, I've got a bridge to sell you.

Snake in the grass.

6.5

满	滿	mǎn	plentiful
载	載	zài	load
而	而	ér	and, then
归	歸	guī	to return

Huge profits. Good returns.

Made a killing.

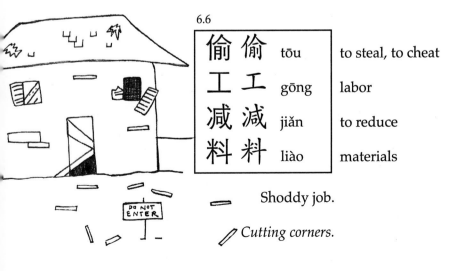

6.6

偷	偷	tōu	to steal, to cheat
工	工	gōng	labor
减	減	jiǎn	to reduce
料	料	liào	materials

Shoddy job.

Cutting corners.

CHARACTER

7

人品

人品

7.1

毕	畢	bì	completely
恭	恭	gōng	to honor
毕	畢	bì	completely
敬	敬	jìng	to respect

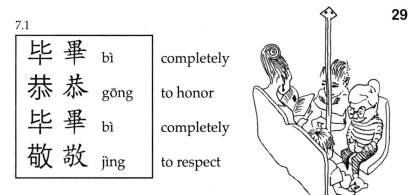

Honor and respect others. (Used to focus
toward elders and teachers.)

Common courtesy.

7.2

待	待	dài	to treat
人	人	rén	person, people
如	如	rú	like
己	己	jǐ	self

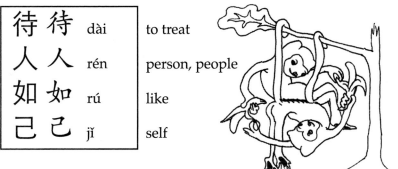

Treat others as you would
like to be treated.

Global Ethic - The Golden Rule

7.3

明	明	míng	to clarify
辨	辨	biàn	to differentiate
是	是	shì	right, yes
非	非	fēi	wrong, no

Clear judgement of right and wrong.

Knowing right from wrong.

Happiness is to help others.

If you're happy, I'm happy.

7.4

助	助	zhù	to help
人	人	rén	person, people
为	為	wéi	to be
乐	樂	lè	happy

7.5

Scam artist. fake

Wolf in sheep's clothing. kindness

fake

righteousness

假	假	jiǎ
仁	仁	rén
假	假	jiǎ
义	義	yì

7.6

勤	勤	qín
劳	勞	láo
苦	苦	kǔ
干	幹	gàn

diligent A hardworking person.

work, labor *Workhorse.*

hardship *Hard work pays off.*

to work, to execute

COLOR CODED

8

颜色类

顏色類

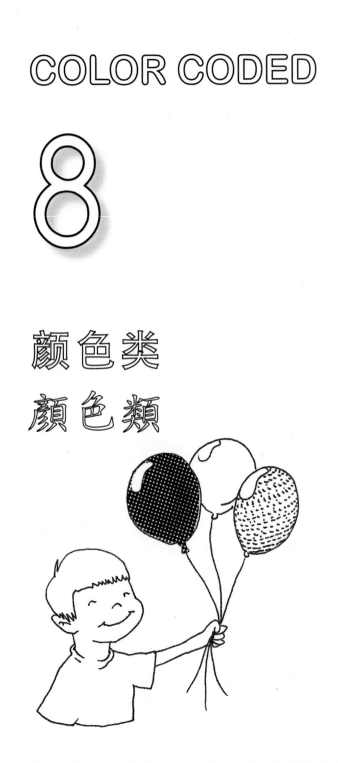

8.1

黑	黑	hēi	black
白	白	bái	white
分	分	fēn	to separate
明	明	míng	clear

Black and white.

Clear and concise. No gray area.

8.2

青	青	qīng	green
出	出	chū	to come out
于	於	yú	from
蓝	藍	lán	blue

The student excels the teacher.

Prodigy. Whiz kid.

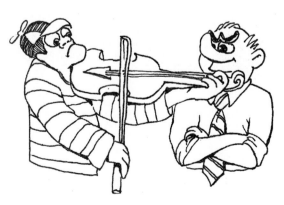

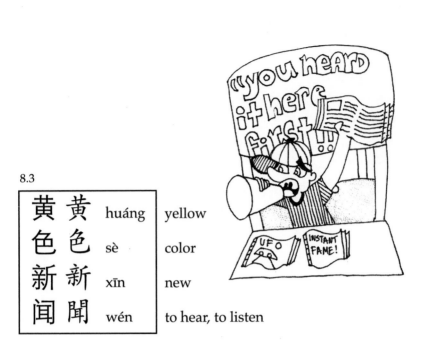

8.3

黄	黄	huáng	yellow
色	色	sè	color
新	新	xīn	new
闻	聞	wén	to hear, to listen

Yellow journalism. Sensational news to attract readers.

Tabloid. Muckraking journalism.

8.4

赤	赤	chì	bare, dark red
诚	誠	chéng	honesty
相	相	xiāng	mutual
待	待	dài	to treat

Mutual respect in utmost sincere manner.

Brotherhood. Sisterhood.

8.5

红	紅	hóng	red
男	男	nán	man
绿	綠	lǜ	green
女	女	nǚ	woman

A well-dressed couple.

Dressed to the nines.

8.6

朱	朱	zhū	bright red
门	門	mén	doors
绣	繡	xiù	embroidered*
户	户	hù	windows

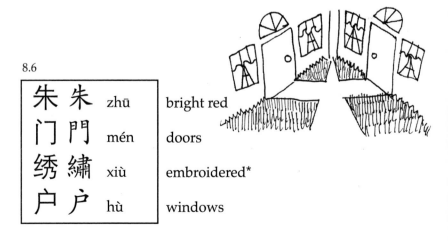

Wealthy families. *Well decorated.

Old money or self-made.

COMMENTS

9

评语

評語

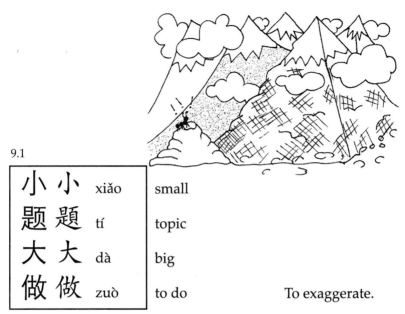

9.1

小	小	xiǎo	small
题	题	tí	topic
大	大	dà	big
做	做	zuò	to do

To exaggerate.

"Making a mountain out of a molehill." - Nicholas Udall

9.2

岂	豈	qǐ	what, how
有	有	yǒu	to have
此	此	cǐ	such
理	理	lǐ	logic, reason

No such thing!

Ridiculous!

9.3

千	千	qiān	thousand
篇	篇	piān	pages
一	一	yí	one
律	律	lǜ	similarity

Repetitive.

Same old. Same old.

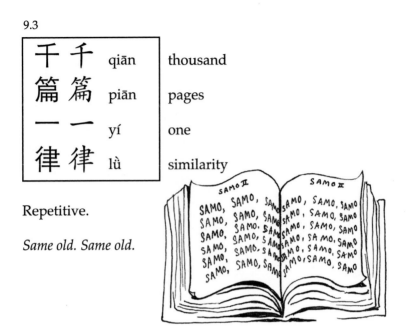

9.4

理	理	lǐ	reason
所	所	suǒ	therefore
当	當	dāng	certain
然	然	rán	so

Absolutely!

Without a doubt.

9.5

业	業	yè	job, occupation
余	餘	yú	beyond, surplus
性	性	xìng	nature
质	質	zhì	quality

Amateurish.

Looks homemade. Sideline.

9.6

莫	莫	mò	no
名	名	míng	name
其	其	qí	that
妙	妙	miào	subtle, scheme

Incomprehensible. Nonsense.

I don't get it.　　　*Gibberish.*

9.7

与	與	yǔ	with
众	衆	zhòng	others
不	不	bù	not
同	同	tóng	same

Unique. Special.

Standout. One of a kind.

9.8

自	自	zì	self, own
作	作	zuò	to act
自	自	zì	self, own
受	受	shòu	to suffer

Self-inflicted.

Shoot oneself in the foot.

9.9

两	兩	liǎng	two, both
袖	袖	xiù	sleeves
清	清	qīng	clean
风	風	fēng	wind

No corruption here.

Nothing up one's sleeve.

Nothing to hide.

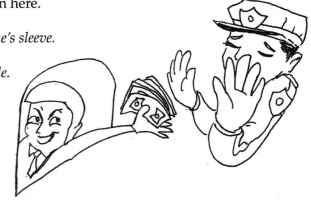

DON'T, UN-, NOT

10

不
不

10.1

不	不	bú	don't
见	見	jiàn	to see
不	不	bú	don't
散	散	sàn	to part, to leave

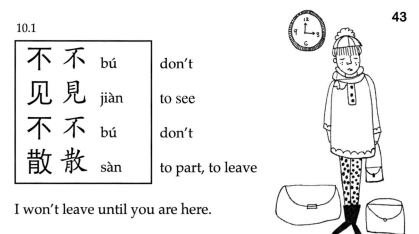

I won't leave until you are here.

Be there! Hang tight!   Don't leave without me.

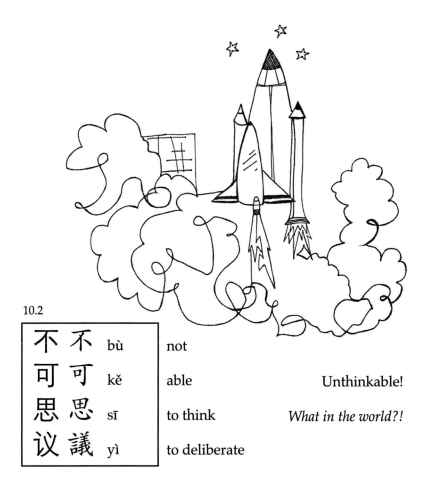

10.2

不	不	bù	not
可	可	kě	able
思	思	sī	to think
议	議	yì	to deliberate

Unthinkable!

What in the world?!

10.3

不	不	bú	not
速	速	sù	to invite
之	之	zhī	of
客	客	kè	guest

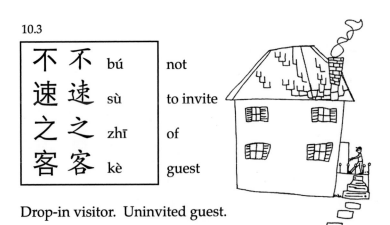

Drop-in visitor. Uninvited guest.

"Look who's here!"   Out of the blue.

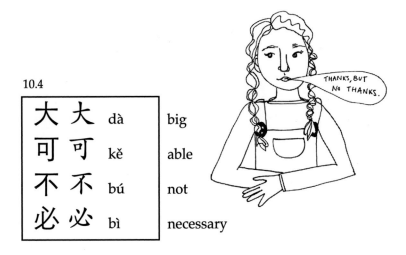

10.4

大	大	dà	big
可	可	kě	able
不	不	bú	not
必	必	bì	necessary

Totally unnecessary. Don't need it.

Thanks, but no thanks.

10.5

不	不	bù	not
打	打	dǎ	to beat
自	自	zì	self
招	招	zhāo	to admit

Voluntary confession.

Cop a plea.

10.6

不	不	bù	not
由	由	yóu	from
自	自	zì	self
主	主	zhǔ	to control

Out of one's hands.

Can't help myself.

DOUBLE DOUBLE

11

叠语

11.1

清	清	qīng
清	清	qīng
楚	楚	chǔ
楚	楚	chǔ

} clear

} concise

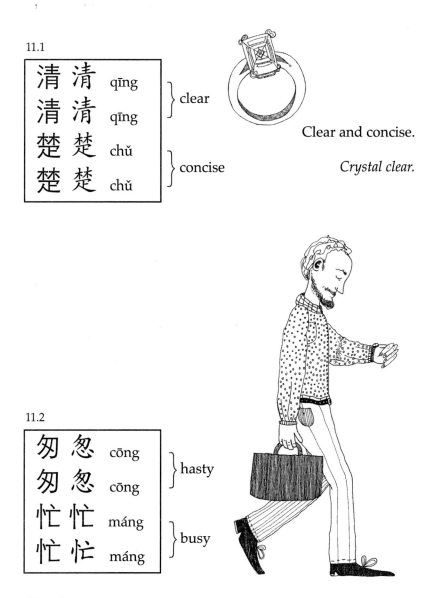

Clear and concise.

Crystal clear.

11.2

匆	忽	cōng
匆	忽	cōng
忙	忙	máng
忙	忙	máng

} hasty

} busy

Very busy.

Busy as a bee.

11.3

随	隨	suí
随	隨	suí
便	便	biàn
便	便	biàn

} to follow

} easy

Anything goes.

Whatever.

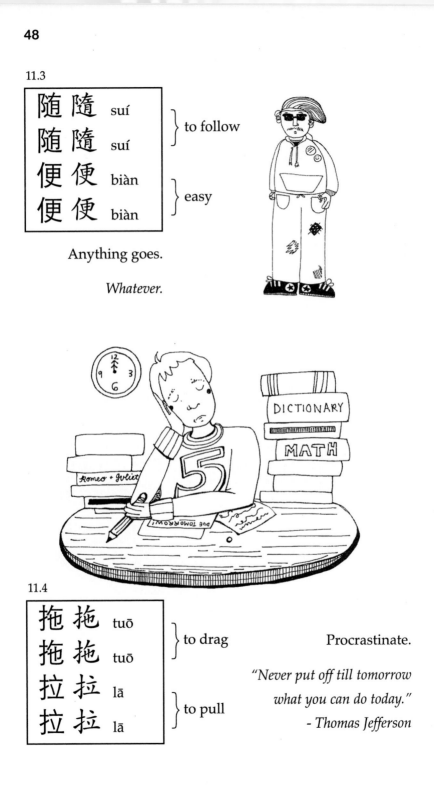

11.4

拖	拖	tuō
拖	拖	tuō
拉	拉	lā
拉	拉	lā

} to drag

} to pull

Procrastinate.

"Never put off till tomorrow
what you can do today."
- Thomas Jefferson

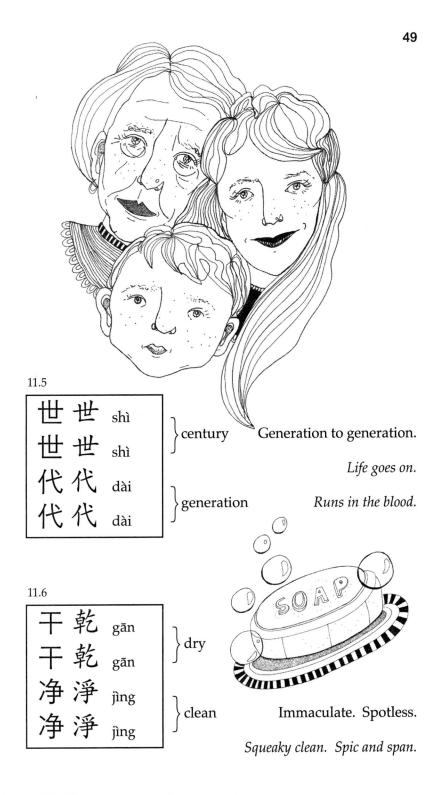

11.5

世	世	shì
世	世	shì
代	代	dài
代	代	dài

} century

} generation

Generation to generation.

Life goes on.

Runs in the blood.

11.6

干	乾	gān
干	乾	gān
净	淨	jìng
净	淨	jìng

} dry

} clean

Immaculate. Spotless.

Squeaky clean. Spic and span.

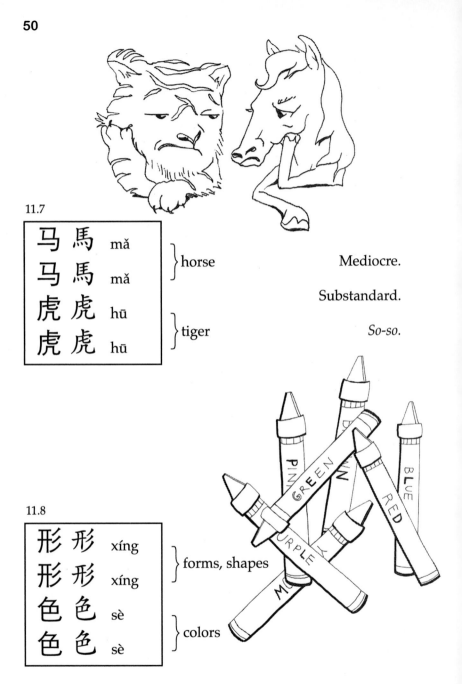

11.7

马	馬	mǎ
马	馬	mǎ
虎	虎	hū
虎	虎	hū

} horse

} tiger

Mediocre.

Substandard.

So-so.

11.8

形	形	xíng
形	形	xíng
色	色	sè
色	色	sè

} forms, shapes

} colors

Colorfully lined.

Variety is the spice of life.

11.9

甜	甜	tián	
甜	甜	tián	} sweet
蜜	蜜	mì	
蜜	蜜	mì	} honey

Sweet as honey.

Lovey dovey. Love is in the air.

EMOTIONS

12

情绪

情緒

12.1

喜	喜	xǐ	happy
怒	怒	nù	angry
哀	哀	āi	sad
乐	樂	lè	joyful

Emotions.

Mood.

12.2

多	多	duō	many
愁	愁	chóu	worries
善	善	shàn	sensitive
感	感	gǎn	feelings

Emotionally sensitive.

Weeping willow.

12.3

同	同	tóng	same
病	病	bìng	illness
相	相	xiāng	mutual
怜	憐	lián	sympathy

Feeling sorry for each other.

Misery loves company.

12.4

走	走	zǒu	to walk
投	投	tóu	to throw, to yield
无	無	wú	no
路	路	lù	road

Dead end. No prospect.

Hit rock bottom.

12.5

怒	怒	nù	angry
发	髮	fà	hair
冲	衝	chōng	to topple
冠	冠	guān	hat

Extremely angry.   *Mad as hell.*

12.6

心	心	xīn	heart
满	满	mǎn	full
意	意	yì	intention
足	足	zú	sufficient

Completely satisfied.

Happy camper. Happy as a clam.

12.7

悲	悲	bēi	sadness
喜	喜	xǐ	joy, happiness
交	交	jiāo	to join
集	集	jí	to gather

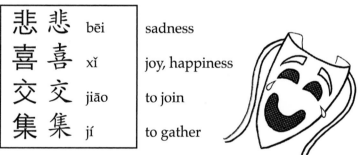

Mixed emotions.

Tears of joy and sorrow.

12.8

面	面	miàn	face
红	红	hóng	red
耳	耳	ěr	ears
赤	赤	chì	dark red

Feeling embarrassed or ashamed.   *Red in the face.*

12.9

心	心	xīn	heart
重	重	zhòng	heavy
如	如	rú	as
铅	鉛	qiān	lead

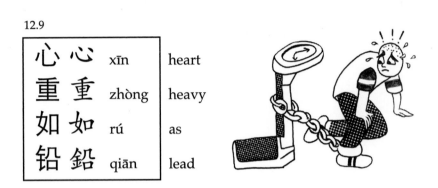

Heavy heart.

I've got that sinking feeling.

12.10

兴	興	xìng	excitement
高	高	gāo	high
采	采	cǎi	spirit
烈	烈	liè	vigorous, strong

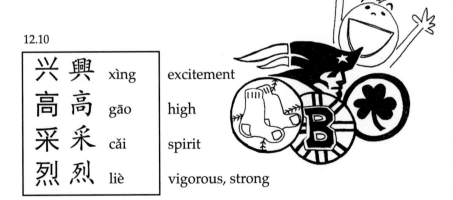

Excitement. All fired up!

Go Bruins, Go Celtics, Go Pats, Go Sox, GO!

12.11

心	心	xīn	heart
血	血	xuè	blood
来	來	lái	to gush
潮	潮	cháo	tides

Act on a whim.

Pumped up! Spur of the moment.

12.12

垂	垂	chuí	to hang low
头	頭	tóu	head
丧	喪	sàng	sad
气	氣	qì	atmosphere

Depressed. Sad.

Feeling down on your luck.

ENCOURAGEMENT

13

鼓励

鼓勵

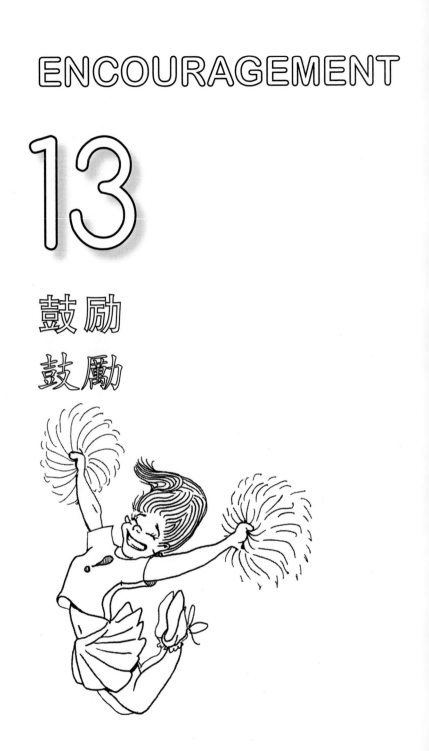

13.1

重	重	chóng	to start over
见	見	jiàn	to see
天	天	tiān	sky
日	日	rì	sun, day

A new beginning!

Tomorrow is another day!

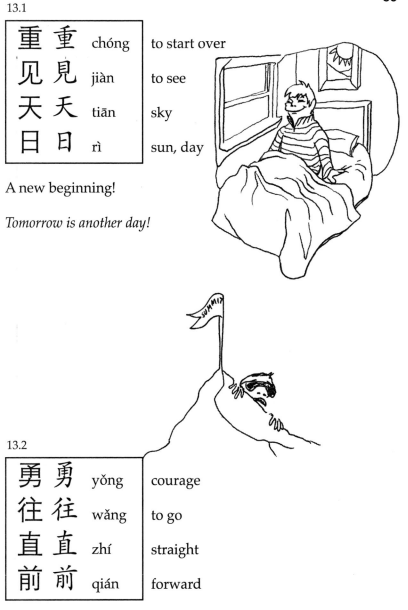

13.2

勇	勇	yǒng	courage
往	往	wǎng	to go
直	直	zhí	straight
前	前	qián	forward

March forward. Have courage.

"Stay the course, light a star,
Change the world where'er you are." - Richard Le Gallienne

With perseverance, everything is possible.

Never give up.

13.3

愚	愚	yú	silly
公	公	gōng	old man
移	移	yí	to move
山	山	shān	mountain

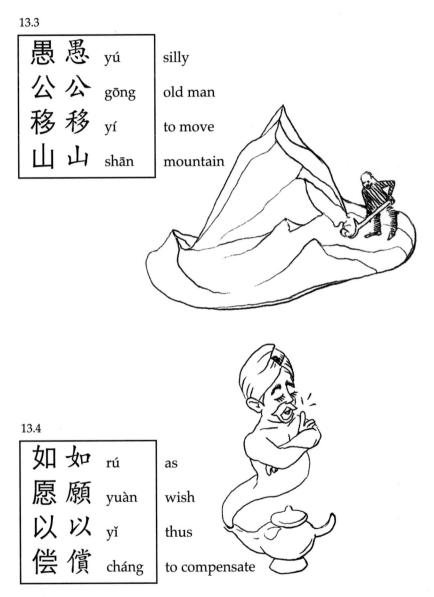

13.4

如	如	rú	as
願	願	yuàn	wish
以	以	yǐ	thus
償	償	cháng	to compensate

Wish is granted.

Dreams come true.

Be hopeful.

Every cloud has a silver lining.

13.5

云	雲	yún	clouds
开	開	kāi	to open
日	日	rì	sun
出	出	chū	to come out

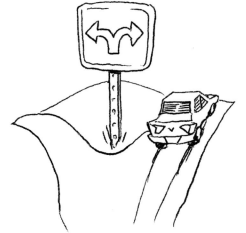

13.6

拿	拿	ná	to take, to hold
定	定	dìng	firm, fixed
主	主	zhǔ	main, important
意	意	yì	idea

Be decisive. Make up your mind.

Don't second guess.

ENVIRONMENT

14

环境
環境

14.1

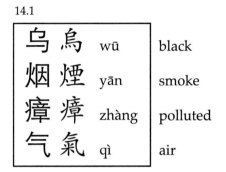

乌	烏	wū	black
烟	煙	yān	smoke
瘴	瘴	zhàng	polluted
气	氣	qì	air

Polluted air.

Ugh! Reach for the masks!

14.2

空	空	kōng	empty
气	氣	qì	air
清	清	qīng	clean
新	新	xīn	fresh

Fresh air.

Breathe in!

14.3

环	環	huán	to encircle
境	境	jìng	surroundings
污	污	wū	dirty
染	染	rǎn	to contaminate

Polluted environment.

EPA at work.

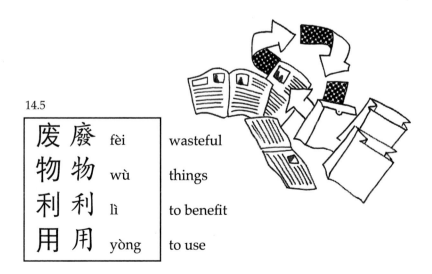

14.4

垃	垃	lā	rubbish
圾	圾	jī	trash
如	如	rú	as
山	山	shān	mountain

Mountains of trash.

Wasteland.

14.5

废	廢	fèi	wasteful
物	物	wù	things
利	利	lì	to benefit
用	用	yòng	to use

Reduce, reuse, recycle.

"One man's trash is another man's treasure." - James Madison

FAMILY VALUES

15

家教
家教

15.1

敬	敬	jìng	to respect
老	老	lǎo	old
慈	慈	cí	to love
幼	幼	yòu	young

Respect the old and love the young.

Get to the basics.

15.2

相	相	xiāng	together
亲	親	qīn	to be intimate
相	相	xiāng	together
爱	愛	ài	to love

To love and embrace each other.

"How do I love thee, let me count the ways."
- Elizabeth Barrett Browning

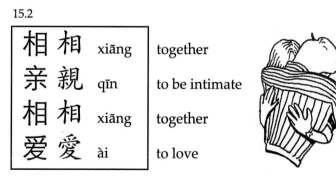

15.3

合	闔	hé	whole
家	家	jiā	family
团	團	tuán	to unite
圆	圓	yuán	together, complete

Family reunion.

Togetherness is a good thing.

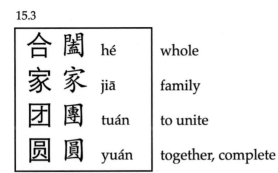

15.4

传	傳	chuán	to pass on
家	家	jiā	family
之	之	zhī	of
宝	寶	bǎo	treasure

Family heirloom.

Valued treasure.

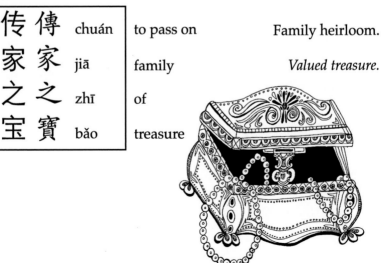

15.5

养	養	yǎng	to give birth to
而	而	ér	yet
不	不	bú	not
教	教	jiào	to teach, to nurture

Irresponsible parenting.

Lack of parental guidance.

15.6

成	成	chéng	to establish	A job and a family.
家	家	jiā	family	*A family man.*
立	立	lì	to build	*Father knows best.*
业	業	yè	business, career	

15.7

母	母	mǔ	mother
女	女	nǚ	daughter
连	連	lián	to connect
心	心	xīn	hearts

Mother-daughter bond.

Unconditional love.

15.8

贤	賢	xián	loving
妻	妻	qī	wife
良	良	liáng	kind
母	母	mǔ	mother

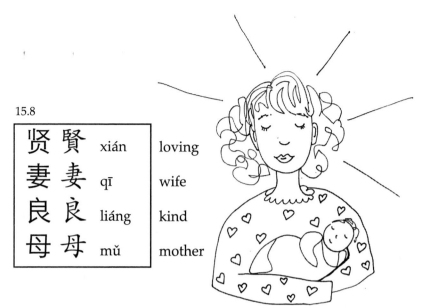

Loving wife and devoted mother.

Behind every great man, there is a great woman.

15.9

倾	傾	qīng	to uproot
家	家	jiā	family
荡	蕩	dàng	to ruin, to reduce
产	產	chǎn	property

Generations of wealth all wiped out.

A family torn apart.

FOOD

16

食物
食物

16.1

饭	飯	fàn	rice	A good meal!
香	香	xiāng	fragrant	*Comfort food.*
菜	菜	cài	meals, vegetables	*Hit the spot.*
甜	甜	tián	sweet	

16.2

淡	淡	dàn	bland	Bland (food).
而	而	ér	and	Not interesting.
无	無	wú	no	*Tepid. Blah!*
味	味	wèi	taste	

16.3

家	家	jiā	family
常	常	cháng	often
便	便	biàn	easy
饭	飯	fàn	meal, rice

Home cooking. Routine, no effort.

Easy as a pie. Piece of cake.

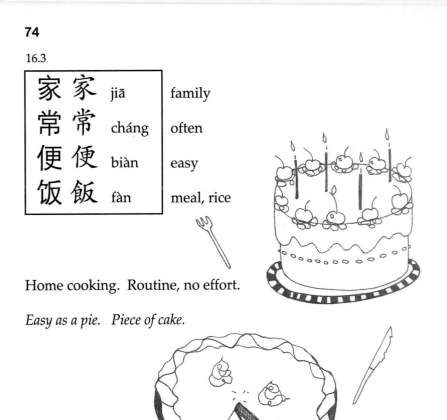

16.4

食	食	shí	food
物	物	wù	things
中	中	zhòng	to fall into
毒	毒	dú	poison

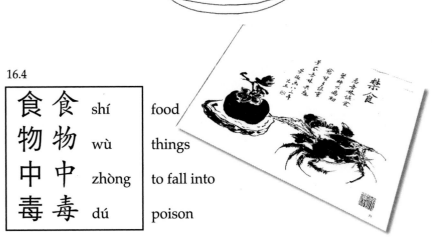

Food poisoning. *Avoid toxic food combinations.*

Beer before liquor never sicker, liquor before beer never fear.

16.5

mouth watering

津	津	jīn
津	津	jīn
有	有	yǒu
味	味	wèi

Delicious. Tasty. to have

Yum yum. taste

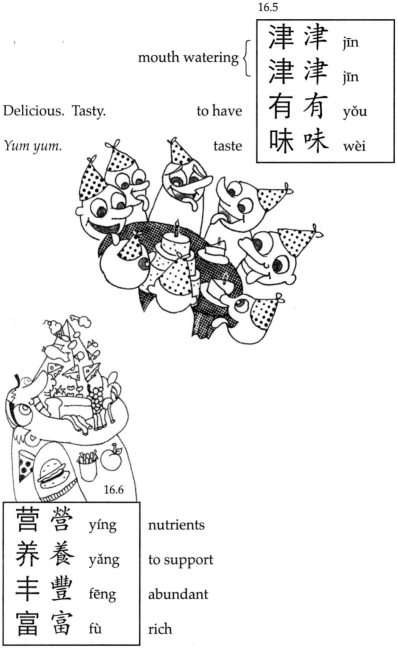

16.6

营	營	yíng	nutrients
养	養	yǎng	to support
丰	豐	fēng	abundant
富	富	fù	rich

Nutritious. *A square meal.*

www.ChooseMyPlate.gov (Replacing the Food Pyramid.)

FRIENDSHIP

友情
友情

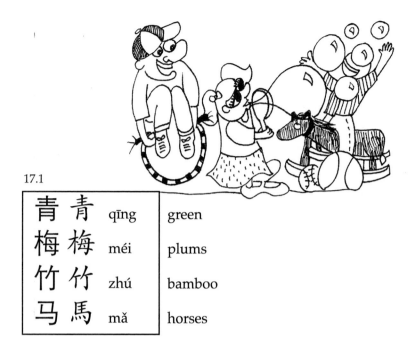

17.1

青	青	qīng	green
梅	梅	méi	plums
竹	竹	zhú	bamboo
马	馬	mǎ	horses

Games children play.

Boys will be boys.   Childhood sweethearts.

17.2

友	友	yǒu	friend
情	情	qíng	feelings
永	永	yǒng	forever
恒	恆	héng	lasting

Long lasting friendship.

Friendship forever.

17.3

老	老	lǎo	old
朋	朋	péng	company
老	老	lǎo	old
友	友	yǒu	friend

Lifelong friends.

"Make new friends but keep the old,
One is silver, the other is gold."
- Girl Scout Camp Song

17.4

酒	酒	jiǔ	alcohol
肉	肉	ròu	meat
朋	朋	péng	company
友	友	yǒu	friend

Beer buddies. (This 'friendship' may
have a negative connotation in different cultures.)

Fair-weather friend. Friends don't let friends drink and drive.

17.5

患	患	huàn	trouble, disaster
难	難	nàn	hardship
之	之	zhī	of
交	交	jiāo	association

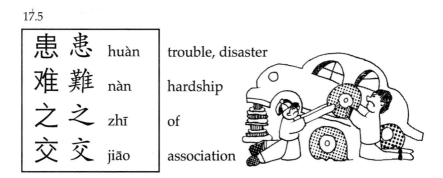

Friendship under difficult times. Allies.

"A friend in need is a friend indeed." - English proverb

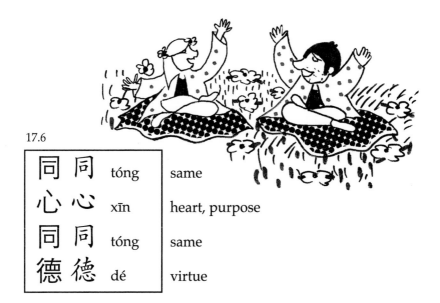

17.6

同	同	tóng	same
心	心	xīn	heart, purpose
同	同	tóng	same
德	德	dé	virtue

In pursuit of the same moral value.

Shared goals.

GENTLEMAN'S AGREEMENT

18

君子协定

君子協定

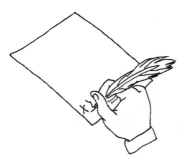

18.1

说	說	shuō	to say
到	到	dào	to reach, to arrive
做	做	zuò	to do, to act
到	到	dào	to reach, to arrive

Do as you say.

Walk the talk.

18.2

说	說	shuō	to say
能	能	néng	able, can
必	必	bì	must be
能	能	néng	able, can

Yes I can!

Put your money where your mouth is.

18.3

说	說	shuō	to say
是	是	shì	yes
必	必	bì	must be
是	是	shì	yes

Keep your promise.

Yes means yes.

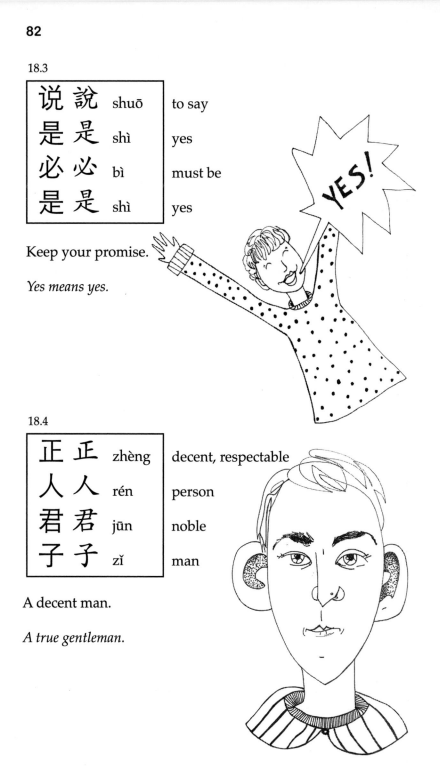

18.4

正	正	zhèng	decent, respectable
人	人	rén	person
君	君	jūn	noble
子	子	zǐ	man

A decent man.

A true gentleman.

18.5

一	一	yì	one
言	言	yán	word
既	既	jì	already
出	出	chū	out
驷	駟	sì	four-horse
马	馬	mǎ	carriage
难	難	nán	difficult
追	追	zhuī	to chase

Even the fastest horses cannot retract a gentleman's word.

Your word is your bond.

GREETINGS

19

贺语
賀語

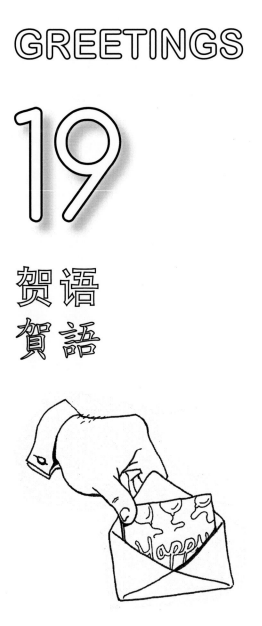

19.1

新	新	xīn	new	
年	年	nián	year	
快	快	kuài	pleased, rapid	
乐	樂	lè	happy	Happy New Year!

Happy New Year!

19.2

生	生	shēng	birth
日	日	rì	date
快	快	kuài	pleased, rapid
乐	樂	lè	happy

Happy birthday!

Older and wiser.

19.3

万	萬	wàn	tens of thousands
事	事	shì	things, matters
如	如	rú	as
意	意	yì	intention, idea

All things going your way! Good luck!

Everything is coming up roses.

19.4

步	步	bù	} step
步	步	bù	
高	高	gāo	high
升	升	shēng	to rise

Wishing you greater success.

Onward and upward.

19.5

福	福	fú	happiness
禄	禄	lù	compensation
双	雙	shuāng	both
全	全	quán	complete

Wishing you both happiness
and good luck.

Double happiness. 囍

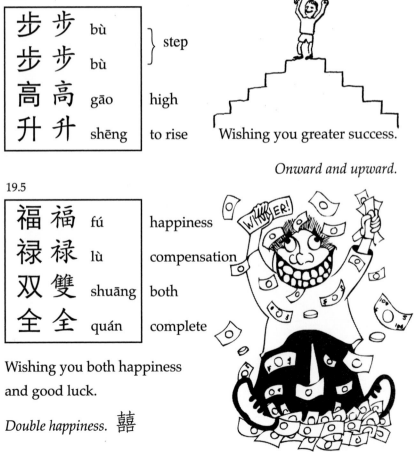

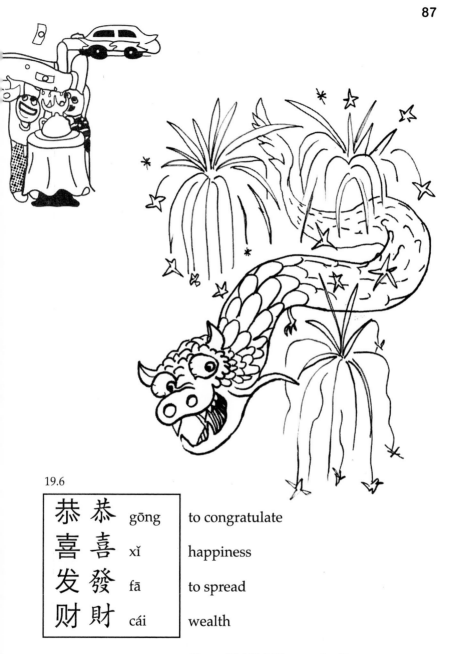

19.6

恭	恭	gōng	to congratulate
喜	喜	xǐ	happiness
发	發	fā	to spread
财	財	cái	wealth

Kung Hei Fat Choy as in Cantonese
dialect during Chinese New Year.

Wishing you a bountiful New Year! Spread good cheer!

HAVE &
HAVE NOT

有 和 无
有 和 無

20.1

有	有	yǒu	to have
头	頭	tóu	head
有	有	yǒu	to have
脑	腦	nǎo	brain

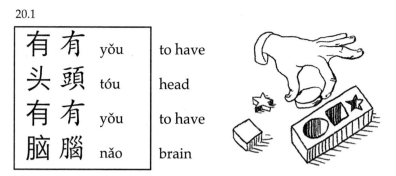

To have common sense. To be sensible and intelligent.

Good head on one's shoulders.

20.2

无	無	wú	to have not
家	家	jiā	home
可	可	kě	can
归	歸	guī	to return

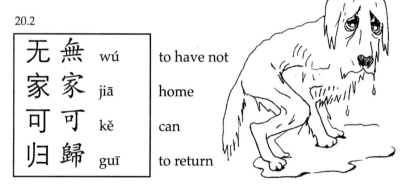

Homeless. *No roof over one's head.*

Support your local Humane Society.

20.3

有	有	yǒu	to have
心	心	xīn	heart, intention
无	無	wú	to have not
力	力	lì	ability, energy

Feeling helpless.

The spirit is willing, but the flesh is weak.

20.4

有	有	yǒu	to have
条	條	tiáo	order
有	有	yǒu	to have
理	理	lǐ	logic

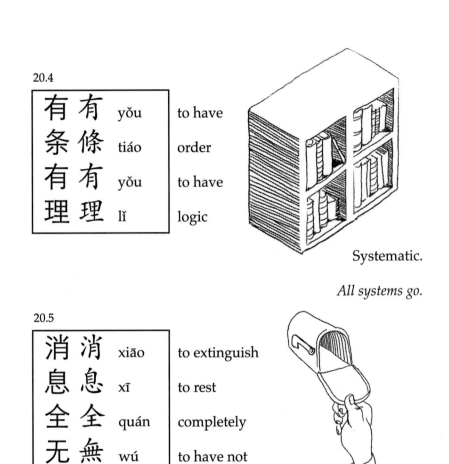

Systematic.

All systems go.

20.5

消	消	xiāo	to extinguish
息	息	xī	to rest
全	全	quán	completely
无	無	wú	to have not

No information. No news.

No news is good news. Waiting with bated breath.

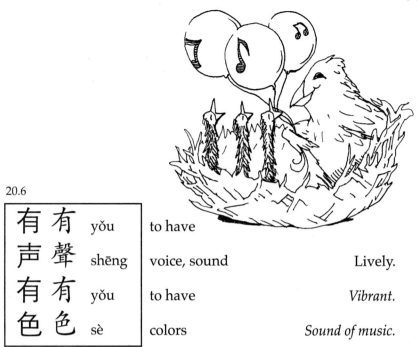

20.6

有	有	yǒu	to have	
声	聲	shēng	voice, sound	Lively.
有	有	yǒu	to have	*Vibrant.*
色	色	sè	colors	*Sound of music.*

20.7

有	有	yǒu	to have
损	損	sǔn	loss, damage
无	無	wú	no
益	益	yì	gain

No gain, but pain.

Nothing to gain but everything to lose.

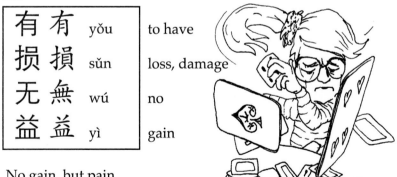

HEAVEN & EARTH

21

天和地
天和地

21.1

天	天	tiān	heaven
差	差	chā	difference
地	地	dì	earth
别	別	bié	apart

A huge difference.

Like night and day.

21.2

天	天	tiān	sky, heaven
罗	羅	luó	baskets
地	地	dì	ground, earth
网	網	wǎng	wires, nets

Surveillance.

Homeland Security.

"You can run, but you can't hide."
- American boxer Joe Louis

21.3

天	天	tiān	heaven
地	地	dì	earth
良	良	liáng	good, kind
心	心	xīn	heart

To have a conscience.

"Always let your conscience be your guide." - Jiminy Cricket

21.4

天	天	tiān	heaven
灾	災	zāi	disasters
人	人	rén	human
祸	禍	huò	misfortune

Human suffering from natural disasters.

Nature's fury.

21.5

谢	謝	xiè	to thank
天	天	tiān	heaven
谢	謝	xiè	to thank
地	地	dì	earth

Be thankful!

Thank goodness! Thank God!

Leave it to God. Let it be.

"Let nature take its course."
- Peter B. Kyne

21.6

听	聽	tīng	to listen
天	天	tiān	heaven
由	由	yóu	accordingly
命	命	mìng	fate

HERE & THERE

22

来和去
來和去

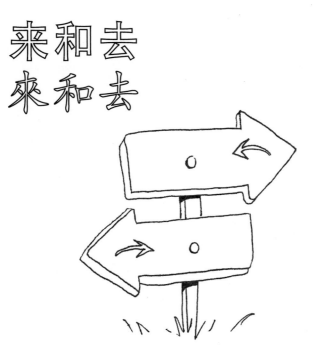

22.1

来	來	lái
来	來	lái
去	去	qù
去	去	qù

} to come, this way

} to go, that way

Describing crowds
and heavy traffic.

Non-stop.

22.2

扭	扭	niǔ	to twist
来	來	lái	this way
扭	扭	niǔ	to twist
去	去	qù	that way

Twisting back and forth.

Follow the music!

22.3

滚	滾	gǔn	to roll
来	來	lái	this way
滚	滾	gǔn	to roll
去	去	qù	that way

Rolling back and forth.

Tumble along.

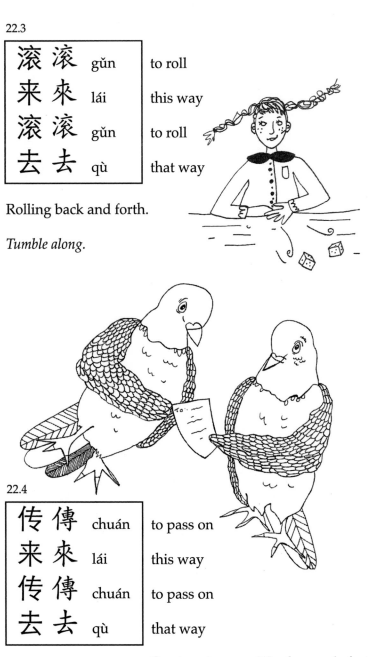

22.4

传	傳	chuán	to pass on
来	來	lái	this way
传	傳	chuán	to pass on
去	去	qù	that way

Carrier pigeons. Word spreads fast.

A little bird told me so. Word on the street.

22.5

说	說	shuō	to talk, to speak
来	來	lái	this way
说	說	shuō	to talk, to speak
去	去	qù	that way

Loves to talk.

Big mouth.

22.6

飘	飄	piāo	to scatter, to float
来	來	lái	this way
飘	飄	piāo	to scatter, to float
去	去	qù	that way

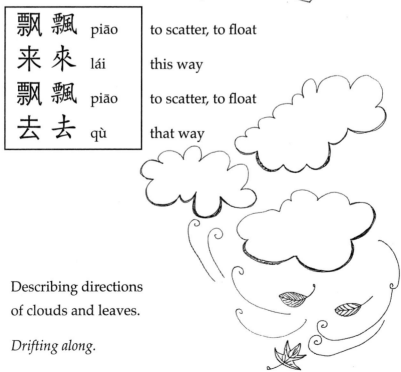

Describing directions of clouds and leaves.

Drifting along.

KEEPING UP

23

相比
相比

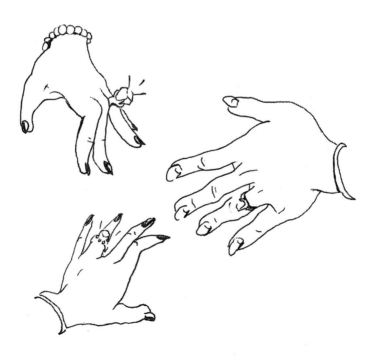

23.1

你	你	nǐ	you
比	比	bǐ	to compare
我	我	wǒ	I
比	比	bǐ	to compare

To compare with each other.

"Keeping up with the Joneses."
- Cartoonist Arthur R. "Pop" Momand

23.2

比	比	bǐ	to compare
上	上	shàng	up
不	不	bù	not
足	足	zú	enough

To compare with those with
wealth, I don't have enough.

"Less is more."
- American architect
Ludwig Mies van der Rohe

23.3

比	比	bǐ	to compare
下	下	xià	down
有	有	yǒu	to have
余	餘	yú	excess

To compare with the less
fortunate, I have too much.

Contentment is the key to happiness.

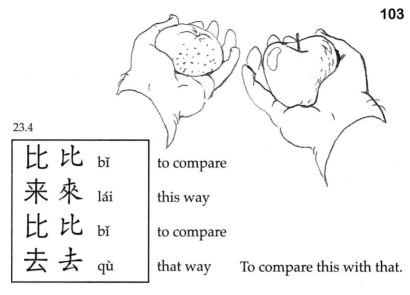

23.4

比	比	bǐ	to compare
来	來	lái	this way
比	比	bǐ	to compare
去	去	qù	that way

To compare this with that.

You can't compare apples to oranges.

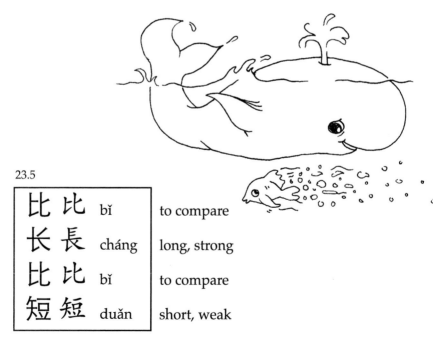

23.5

比	比	bǐ	to compare
长	長	cháng	long, strong
比	比	bǐ	to compare
短	短	duǎn	short, weak

To compare strengths and weaknesses.

May use for measurement.

Competition leads to progress.

LIFE & LIVING

24

生活
生活

24.1

人	人	rén	person
生	生	shēng	life
如	如	rú	like
梦	夢	mèng	dream

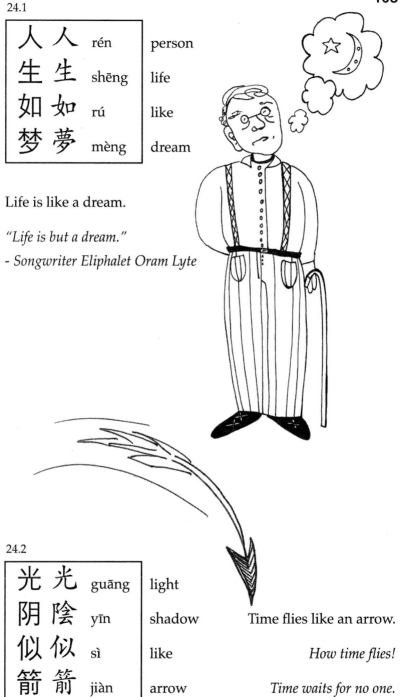

Life is like a dream.

"Life is but a dream."
- Songwriter Eliphalet Oram Lyte

24.2

光	光	guāng	light
阴	陰	yīn	shadow
似	似	sì	like
箭	箭	jiàn	arrow

Time flies like an arrow.

How time flies!

Time waits for no one.

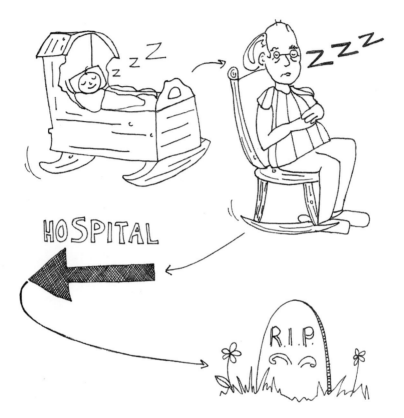

24.3

生	生	shēng	birth
老	老	lǎo	aging
病	病	bìng	sickness
死	死	sǐ	death

Life's predictable path.

Ashes to ashes, dust to dust.

"The seven ages of man."
- William Shakespeare

Fashion of the time.

Trend.

*"Here today,
gone tomorrow."*
- American proverb

24.4

风	風	fēng	wind, to circulate
行	行	xíng	walks, to accept
一	一	yì	one
时	時	shí	time, period

24.5

生	生	shēng	life
不	不	bù	no
逢	逢	féng	to come upon
时	時	shí	in time

LINE STARTS HERE

Good time in life
has not yet arrived.

Wait your turn!

24.6

生	生	shēng	life
离	離	lí	to leave
死	死	sǐ	death
别	別	bié	to part

Saying good-bye in life
is as difficult as in death.

"Parting is such sweet sorrow."
- William Shakespeare

24.7

酸	酸	suān	sour
甜	甜	tián	sweet
苦	苦	kǔ	bitter
辣	辣	là	hot

Life's different phases.

Life can be bittersweet.

Life is like a box of chocolates.
- based on 1994 movie "Forrest Gump."

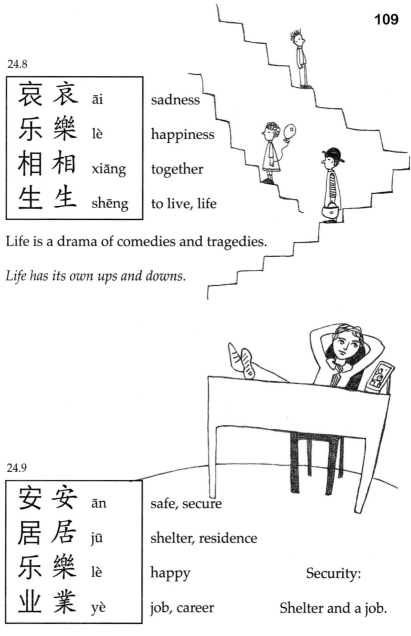

24.8

哀	哀	āi	sadness
乐	樂	lè	happiness
相	相	xiāng	together
生	生	shēng	to live, life

Life is a drama of comedies and tragedies.

Life has its own ups and downs.

24.9

安	安	ān	safe, secure
居	居	jū	shelter, residence
乐	樂	lè	happy
业	業	yè	job, career

Security:

Shelter and a job.

He's got it made.

LOVE & MARRIAGE

爱情和婚姻
愛情和婚姻

25.1

郎	郎	láng	man, groom
才	才	cái	ability, talent
女	女	nǚ	woman, bride
貌	貌	mào	looks, appearance

A well matched couple.

Marriage made in heaven.

25.2

谈	談	tán	to talk
情	情	qíng	feelings
说	說	shuō	to speak
爱	愛	ài	love

A couple in love.

The whole world loves a lover.

25.3

门	門	mén	the door
当	當	dāng	to suit
户	戶	hù	the window
对	對	duì	to fit

Families of same social and economic background.

Good match. Mr. and Mrs. Right.

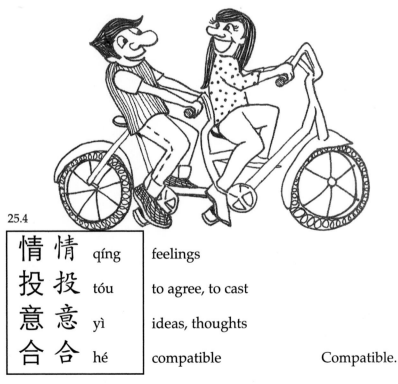

25.4

情	情	qíng	feelings
投	投	tóu	to agree, to cast
意	意	yì	ideas, thoughts
合	合	hé	compatible

Compatible.

Made for each other.

25.5

花	花	huā	flowers
好	好	hǎo	good, in full bloom
月	月	yuè	the moon
圓	圓	yuán	full

Blessings to the newly-weds.

Live happily ever after...

25.6

夫	夫	fū	husband
唱	唱	chàng	to sing
妇	婦	fù	wife
随	隨	suí	to follow

A happy, well adjusted couple.

Soulmate, lifelong bond.

It takes two to tango.

25.7

白	白	bái	white
头	頭	tóu	head
偕	偕	xié	companionship
老	老	lǎo	old age

Growing old together.
Blessings to the newly-weds.

"Till death do us part."
-Book of Common Prayer

25.8

嫁	嫁	jià	to marry
鸡	雞	jī	a chicken
随	隨	suí	to follow
鸡	雞	jī	a chicken
嫁	嫁	jià	to marry
狗	狗	gǒu	a dog
随	隨	suí	to follow
狗	狗	gǒu	a dog

Marry a chicken, lead a chicken's life.

Marry a dog, lead a dog's life.

Make the best out of a marriage.

You've made your bed, now lie in it.

Go along to get along.

NEITHER, NOR

不，非，没
不，非，没

26.1

不	不	bù	neither
冷	冷	lěng	cold
不	不	bú	nor
热	熱	rè	hot

No emotions.

Neither cold nor hot (sense of touch).

Lukewarm.

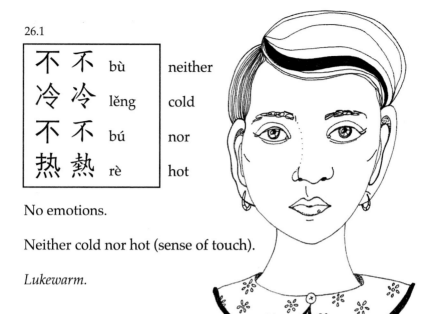

26.2

不	不	bú	neither
痛	痛	tòng	painful
不	不	bù	nor
痒	癢	yǎng	itchy

To be indifferent.

No skin off one's back.

26.3

啼	啼	tí	to cry
笑	笑	xiào	to laugh
皆	皆	jiē	all
非	非	fēi	none

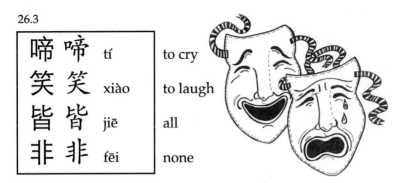

Don't know how to react.

Not sure whether to laugh or cry.

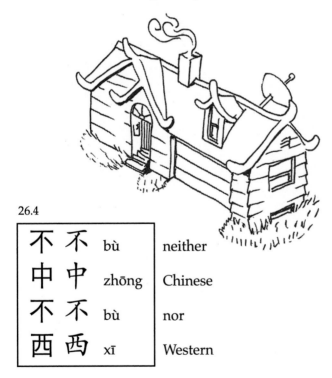

26.4

不	不	bù	neither
中	中	zhōng	Chinese
不	不	bù	nor
西	西	xī	Western

Neither Chinese nor Western
(In fashion, trend and culture).

Neither fish nor fowl. Identity crisis.

26.5

没	没	méi	neither
大	大	dà	big, adult
没	没	méi	nor
小	小	xiǎo	small, child

Lack of respect and understanding for elders.

Generation gap.

26.6

不	不	bù	neither
古	古	gǔ	classic
不	不	bù	nor
今	今	jīn	contemporary

Poor imitation. *Fake. Not the genuine article.*

26.7

没	没	méi	neither
头	頭	tóu	head
没	没	méi	nor
脑	腦	nǎo	brain

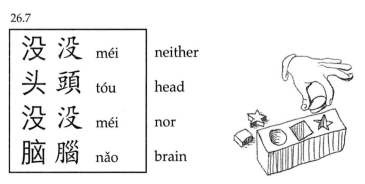

No brain. *Empty head.*

NONE

27

27.1

无	無	wú	no
话	話	huà	word
可	可	kě	can
说	說	shuō	to speak

Nothing more to say.

Speechless. Cat got your tongue.

27.2

无	無	wú	no
话	話	huà	word
不	不	bù	not
谈	談	tán	to say, to discuss

Talk about every subject. *Everything under the sun.*

27.3

无	無	wú	no
奇	奇	qí	strange, curious
不	不	bù	not
有	有	yǒu	to have

Everything imaginable.

Magical.

27.4

无	無	wú	no
头	頭	tóu	head, beginning
无	無	wú	no
尾	尾	wěi	tail, end

No clue.

Can't make heads or tails of it.

27.5

无	無	wú	no
翼	翼	yì	wings
而	而	ér	and yet
飞	飛	fēi	to fly

Vanished without a trace.

Gone in a puff of smoke.

27.6

无	無	wú	no
关	關	guān	to relate
紧	緊	jǐn	tight, urgent
要	要	yào	important, to be in need

Not important.

No big deal.

27.7

无	無	wú	no
法	法	fǎ	law
无	無	wú	no
天	天	tiān	heaven

Lawless.   *Wild.*

27.8

无	無	wú	no
所	所	suǒ	therefore
不	不	bù	not
能	能	néng	possible

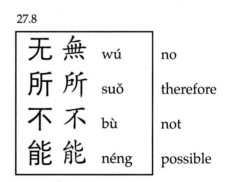

Nothing is impossible.   *Everything is possible.*   *Sky's the limit.*

The United States' Apollo 11 was the first manned mission to land on the moon on July 20, 1969.

27.8

27.9

无	無	wú	no
声	聲	shēng	sound
无	無	wú	no
息	息	xī	breathing

Dead quiet. *So quiet you could hear a pin drop.*

NUMBERS GAME

28

数字
数字

28.1

千	千	qiān	thousands of
方	方	fāng	ways
百	百	bǎi	hundreds of
计	計	jì	plans

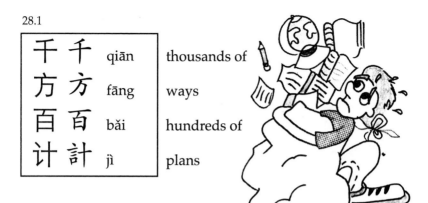

Doing everything possible.

Doing my best. No stone unturned.

28.2

乱	亂	luàn	disorderly
七	七	qī	seven
八	八	bā	eight
糟	糟	zāo	mess

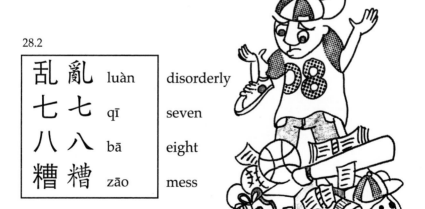

Getting things all mixed up.

Messy, sloppy. Topsy-turvy.

28.3

半	半	bàn	half
斤	斤	jīn	pound*
八	八	bā	eight
两	兩	liǎng	ounces*

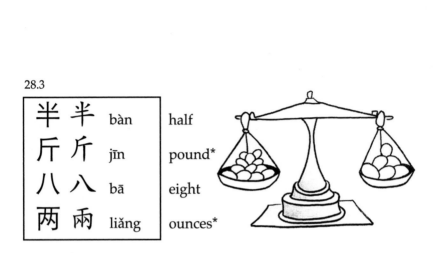

*Unit of weight by old Chinese scale.

Same, no difference.   *Six of one, half a dozen of the other.*

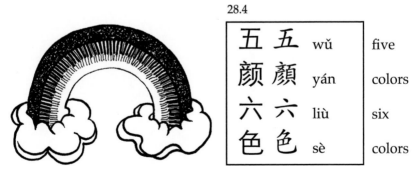

28.4

五	五	wǔ	five
颜	顏	yán	colors
六	六	liù	six
色	色	sè	colors

Variety of colors.

Rainbow colors.   Riot of color.

28.5

百	百	bǎi	a hundred
发	發	fā	to shoot
百	百	bǎi	a hundred
中	中	zhòng	on target

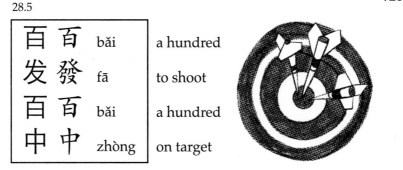

On target. *Bull's eye.*

28.6

三	三	sān	three
思	思	sī	to deliberate
而	而	ér	then
行	行	xíng	to act

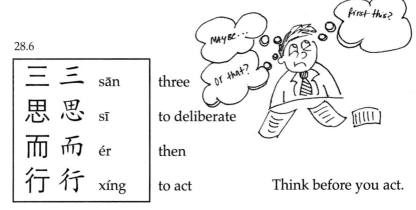

Think before you act.

Look before you leap.

28.7

数	數	shǔ	to count
一	一	yī	No. 1
数	數	shǔ	to count
二	二	èr	No. 2

Extraordinary! Top two.

Cream of the crop. Top of the heap.

28.8

十	十	shí	ten
年	年	nián	years
树	樹	shù	to grow
木	木	mù	tree

It takes ten years for a tree to grow. It takes more years to cultivate a person's character.

It takes a village to raise a child. - African proverb

百	百	bǎi	hundred
年	年	nián	years
树	樹	shù	to cultivate
人	人	rén	person

Rome wasn't built in a day.

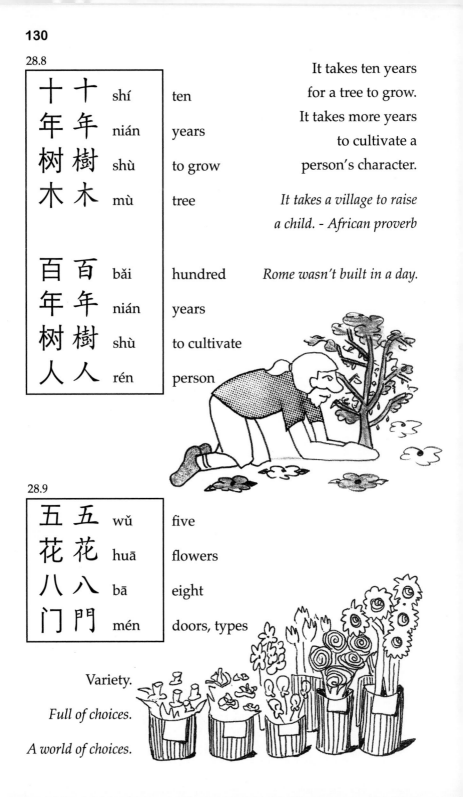

28.9

五	五	wǔ	five
花	花	huā	flowers
八	八	bā	eight
门	門	mén	doors, types

Variety.

Full of choices.

A world of choices.

28.10

千	千	qiān	thousands
言	言	yán	words
万	萬	wàn	tens of thousands
语	語	yǔ	words

Loquacious.

So much to say, so little time to say it.

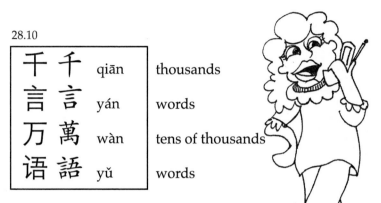

28.11

不	不	bù	neither
三	三	sān	three
不	不	bú	nor
四	四	sì	four

Improper.

Out of line.

OLD AGE

29

老年
老年

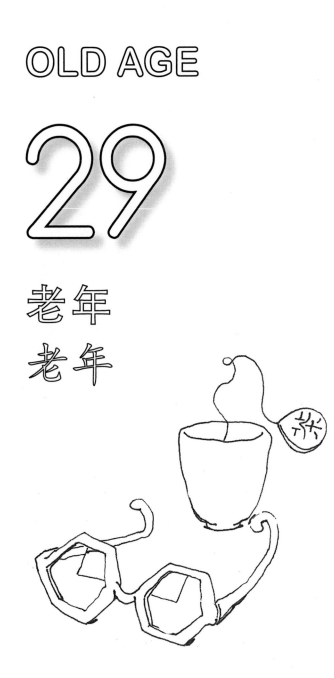

29.1

返	返	fǎn	to reverse
老	老	lǎo	old age
还	還	huán	to return to
童	童	tóng	childhood

An elderly person with
    youthful vitality.

Youth is a state of mind.
        Young at heart.

29.2

人	人	rén	person
老	老	lǎo	old
体	體	tǐ	body
健	健	jiàn	healthy

Old yet physically fit.

Fitness guru.

Forgetful. Memory lapse.

Memory like a sieve.

29.3

前	前	qián	before, just
说	說	shuō	to speak
后	後	hòu	after, soon
忘	忘	wàng	to forget

29.4

慢	慢	màn	slow
手	手	shǒu	hands
慢	慢	màn	slow
脚	腳	jiǎo	feet

Slow movement.

Slow as molasses.

Picture of youth.

You are only as old as you feel.

Age is only a number.

29.5

鹤	鶴	hè	crane
发	髮	fà	hair
童	童	tóng	child
颜	顏	yán	face

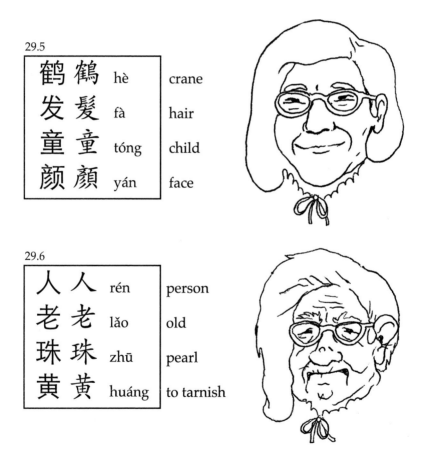

29.6

人	人	rén	person
老	老	lǎo	old
珠	珠	zhū	pearl
黄	黃	huáng	to tarnish

A person lacks charisma due to aging.
(Used to describe a woman lacking charm due to aging.)

An old prune.

PAIRS

30

成对谚语
成對諺語

30.1

触	觸	chù	to touch, to see
景	景	jǐng	sights
生	生	shēng	to arouse
情	情	qíng	sentiments
睹	睹	dǔ	to see
物	物	wù	things
思	思	sī	to remember
人	人	rén	person

Nostalgia.

Down memory lane.

30.2

鹤	鶴	hè	crane
蚌	蚌	bàng	oyster
相	相	xiāng	together
争	爭	zhēng	to fight
渔	漁	yú	fishing
翁	翁	wēng	old man
得	得	dé	to receive, to gain
利	利	lì	benefit, advantage

Third party
winner.

When two dogs fight over a bone, a third one carries it away.

30.3

不	不	bù	not
鸣	鳴	míng	to sound
则	則	zé	then
已	已	yǐ	to cease
一	一	yì	once
鸣	鳴	míng	to make sound
惊	驚	jīng	to surprise
人	人	rén	person, people

Instant fame.

Rocket rise to stardom.

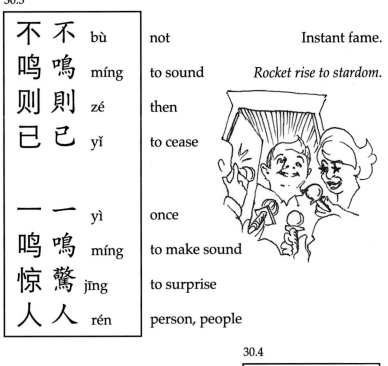

30.4

		to wish		希	希	xī
		to expect		望	望	wàng
		the most		越	越	yuè
		high		高	高	gāo
		to lose		失	失	shī
		hope		望	望	wàng
		the most		越	越	yuè
		big		大	大	dà

The higher the expectation, the greater the disappointment.

30.5

善	善	shàn	to do good
有	有	yǒu	to have
善	善	shàn	good
报	報	bào	reward
恶	惡	è	to be evil
有	有	yǒu	to have
恶	惡	è	bad
报	報	bào	omen

Believe in karma.

What goes around comes around.

Be careful what you wish for.

Don't set your hopes too high.

30.4

30.6

祸	禍	huò	danger
不	不	bù	does not
单	單	dān	single, alone
行	行	xíng	to go
福	福	fú	good luck
无	無	wú	does not
双	雙	shuāng	twice
至	至	zhì	to arrive

Bad luck does not come just once,
Good luck does not happen twice.

Bad luck comes in threes.

30.7

病	病	bìng	sickness
从	從	cóng	from
口	口	kǒu	mouth
入	入	rù	to enter
祸	禍	huò	damage
从	從	cóng	from
口	口	kǒu	mouth
出	出	chū	to go out

30.8

知	知	zhī	to know
易	易	yì	easy
行	行	xíng	to act
难	難	nán	difficult
知	知	zhī	to know
难	難	nán	difficult
行	行	xíng	to act
易	易	yì	easy

Looks easy,
doing it is difficult.

"The devil is in the details."
- American architect
Ludwig Mies van der Rohe

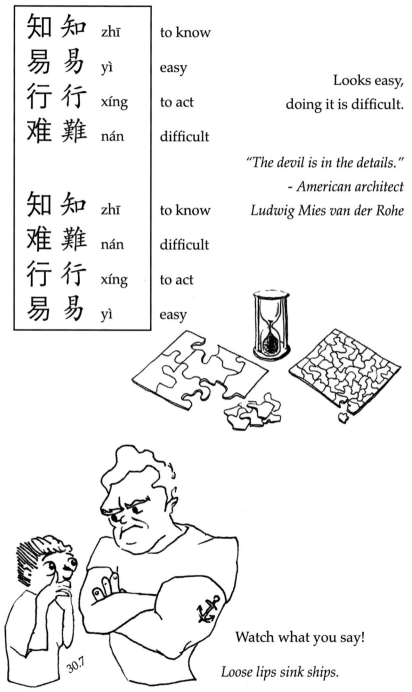

Watch what you say!

Loose lips sink ships.

30.7

30.9

生	生	shēng	to be born
不	不	bú	not
带	帶	dài	to bring
来	來	lái	to come

Worldly possessions are only as temporary as life itself.

死	死	sǐ	to die
不	不	bú	not
带	帶	dài	to bring
去	去	qù	to go

You can't take it with you.

30.10

近	近	jìn	to be close to
朱	朱	zhū	red ink
者	者	zhě	the person
赤	赤	chì	dark red

近	近	jìn	to be close to
墨	墨	mò	black ink
者	者	zhě	the person
黑	黑	hēi	black

Easily influenced.
Peer pressure.

Monkey see, monkey do.

Copycat.

30.11

有	有	yǒu	to have
福	福	fú	happiness
同	同	tóng	together
享	享	xiǎng	to enjoy
有	有	yǒu	to have
祸	禍	huò	misfortune
同	同	tóng	together
当	當	dāng	to bear

Sharing happiness
and worries together.

*Shared joy
is a double joy;
shared sorrow
is half a sorrow.*

- Swedish proverb

30.12

种	種	zhòng	to sow
瓜	瓜	guā	melons
得	得	dé	to harvest
瓜	瓜	guā	melons
种	種	zhòng	to sow
豆	豆	dòu	beans, peas
得	得	dé	to harvest
豆	豆	dòu	beans, peas

You are responsible
for your own action.

You reap what you sow.

PERSONALITY

31

个性
個性

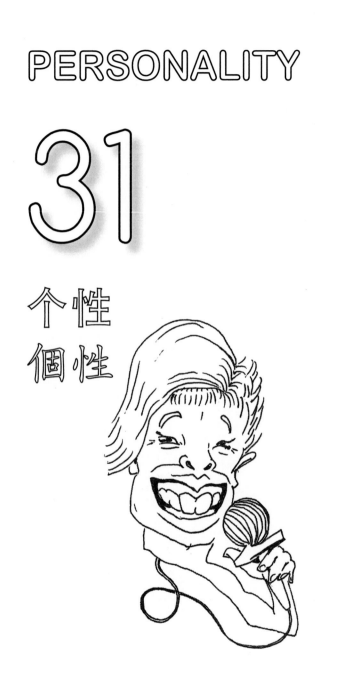

Innocent
and loveable.

31.1

天	天	tiān	natural, heaven	*Natural.*
真	真	zhēn	true, real	*Little darlings.*
烂	爛	làn	bright	
漫	漫	màn	to surge	

31.2

多	多	duō	many
嘴	嘴	zuǐ	mouths
多	多	duō	many
舌	舌	shé	tongues

Gossipy.

Busy body.

31.3

拖	拖	tuō	to drag
泥	泥	ní	mud
带	带	dài	to bring
水	水	shuǐ	water

Wishy-washy.

Not straight forward.

Beating around the bush.

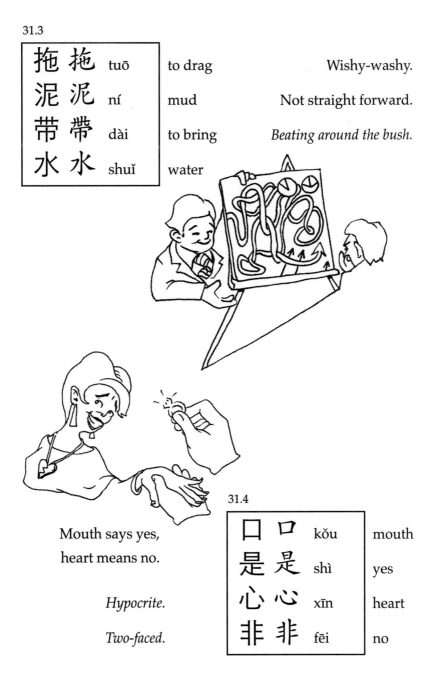

Mouth says yes,
heart means no.

Hypocrite.

Two-faced.

31.4

口	口	kǒu	mouth
是	是	shì	yes
心	心	xīn	heart
非	非	fēi	no

31.5

胆	膽	dǎn	gall
大	大	dà	big
心	心	xīn	heart
细	細	xì	cautious

Brave and careful.

Fortune favors the brave.

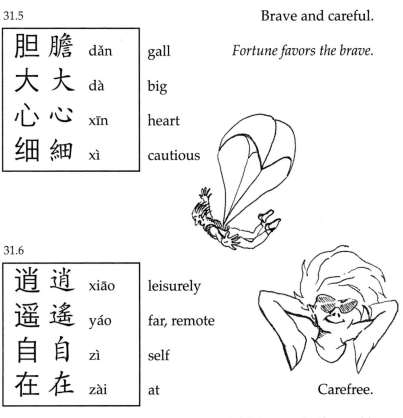

31.6

逍	逍	xiāo	leisurely
遥	遙	yáo	far, remote
自	自	zì	self
在	在	zài	at

Carefree.

Not a care in the world.

31.7

孤	孤	gū	alone
芳	芳	fāng	fame
自	自	zì	self
赏	賞	shǎng	to admire

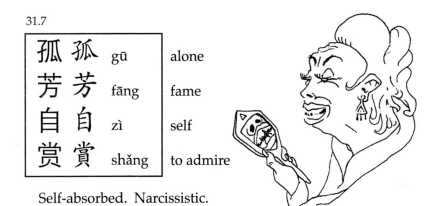

Self-absorbed. Narcissistic.

I, me, my, mine.

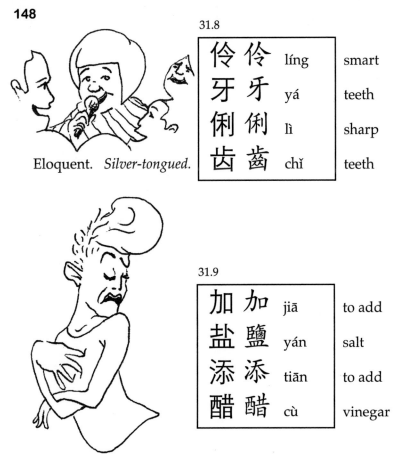

31.8

伶	伶	líng	smart
牙	牙	yá	teeth
俐	俐	lì	sharp
齿	齒	chǐ	teeth

Eloquent. *Silver-tongued.*

31.9

加	加	jiā	to add
盐	鹽	yán	salt
添	添	tiān	to add
醋	醋	cù	vinegar

To exaggerate. To boast. *He's full of it. Full of hot air.*

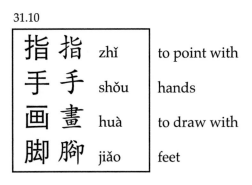

31.10

指	指	zhǐ	to point with
手	手	shǒu	hands
画	畫	huà	to draw with
脚	腳	jiǎo	feet

Intrusive, unwanted advice. Excessive body language.

Butt heads. Backseat drivers.

31.11

诚	誠	chéng	honest
实	實	shí	sincere
可	可	kě	able
靠	靠	kào	to rely on

Reliable.   Trustworthy.

He's good.   *A good egg.*

31.12

斤	斤	jīn	pound
斤	斤	jīn	by pound
计	計	jì	to haggle
较	較	jiào	to compare

Calculating. Enjoys finding fault in petty details.   *Nit-picky.*

31.10

THE POPULAR 'ONE'

32

32.1

一	一	yí	one
窍	竅	qiào	hole
不	不	bù	not
通	通	tōng	to go through

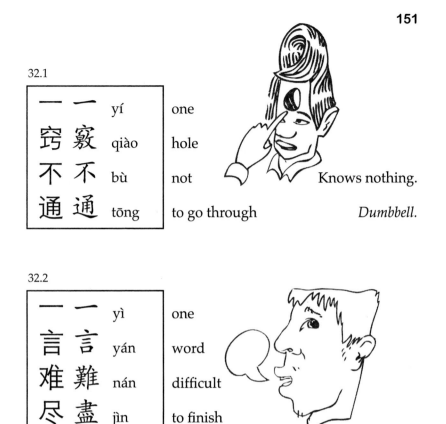

Knows nothing.

Dumbbell.

32.2

一	一	yì	one
言	言	yán	word
难	難	nán	difficult
尽	盡	jìn	to finish

Indescribable.

At a loss for words.

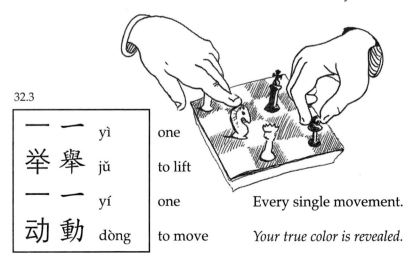

32.3

一	一	yì	one
举	舉	jǔ	to lift
一	一	yí	one
动	動	dòng	to move

Every single movement.

Your true color is revealed.

32.4

一	一	yì	one
文	文	wén	coin
不	不	bù	not
值	值	zhí	worth

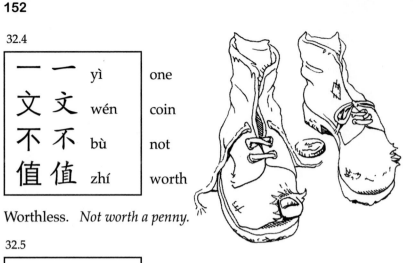

Worthless. *Not worth a penny.*

32.5

一	一	yí	once
见	見	jiàn	to see, to meet
如	如	rú	as
故	故	gù	old friend

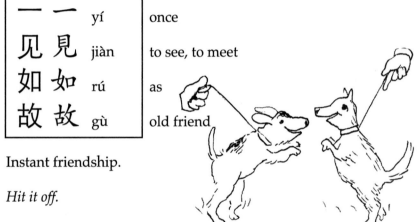

Instant friendship.

Hit it off.

On target. *Right to the point.*

32.6

一	一	yì	one
针	針	zhēn	needle
见	見	jiàn	to see
血	血	xiě	blood

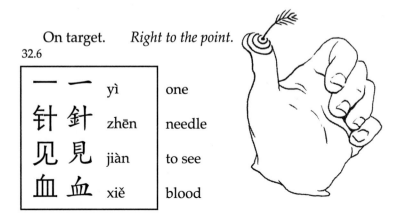

32.7

一	一	yì	one
本	本	běn	book, according to
正	正	zhèng	proper
经	經	jīng	book, guide

Very proper. Be serious.

By the book.

32.8

一	一	yì	one
心	心	xīn	heart
一	一	yí	one
意	意	yì	mind

Very focused. Very sincere.

Undivided attention.

Stingy. A miser.

Cheapskate.

"Hold the purse-strings."
- *James Madison*

32.9

一	一	yì	one
毛	毛	máo	hair
不	不	bù	not
拔	拔	bá	to remove, to pull

PUBLIC NOTICES

33

通告
通告

33.1

不	不	bù	not	No returns. No refunds.
准	准	zhǔn	to allow	*If you break it, you own it.*
退	退	tuì	to return	
货	货	huò	merchandise	

33.2

保	保	bǎo	to keep	
持	持	chí	to hold	Keep quiet.
安	安	ān	peace, calm	*Silence is golden.*
静	静	jìng	quiet	

33.3

禁	禁	jìn	to prohibit
用	用	yòng	to use
手	手	shǒu	hand
机	機	jī	gadget, appliance

No cell phones.

Cell phone is allowed only in designated area.

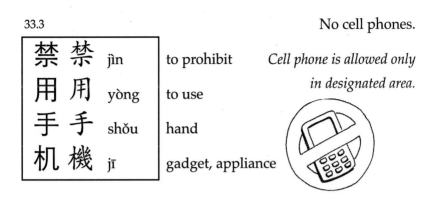

33.4

不	不	bù	not
准	准	zhǔn	to allow
照	照	zhào	to shoot
相	相	xiàng	picture

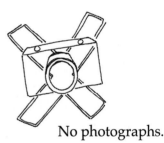

No photographs.

Keep your memories in your brain box!

33.5

禁	禁	jìn	to prohibit
止	止	zhǐ	to stop
饮	飲	yǐn	drinks
食	食	shí	food

No drinks or food.

Drinks and food not allowed.

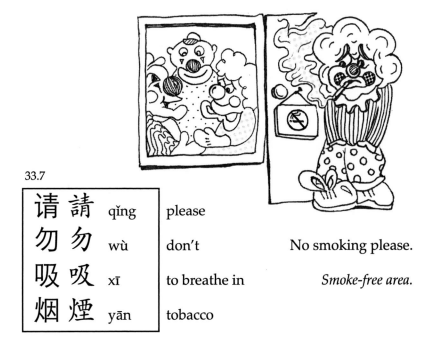

33.6

闲	閒	xián	idle
人	人	rén	person
莫	莫	mò	not
入	入	rù	to enter

Strangers keep out.

No trespassing.

33.7

请	請	qǐng	please
勿	勿	wù	don't
吸	吸	xī	to breathe in
烟	煙	yān	tobacco

No smoking please.

Smoke-free area.

33.8

现	现	xiàn	to present
金	金	jīn	gold, money
交	交	jiāo	to exchange
易	易	yì	to trade

Cash only.

Leave your credit cards at home.

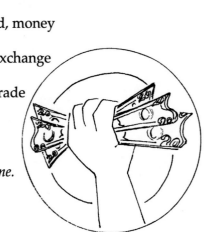

33.9

提	提	dī	to beware
防	防	fáng	to avoid
小	小	xiǎo	small, petty
偷	偷	tōu	thief

Beware of pickpockets.

Watch your wallets.

33.10

通	通	tōng	throughout
宵	宵	xiāo	night
达	達	dá	to reach
旦	旦	dàn	dawn

Twenty-four hour non-stop.

Open 24/7. All day every day.

33.11

风	風	fēng	wind
雨	雨	yǔ	rain
无	無	wú	not
阻	阻	zǔ	to prohibit, to stop

Rain or shine, we are here for you!

Open no matter what.

33.12

请	請	qǐng	please
勿	勿	wù	do not
吐	吐	tǔ	to spit
痰	痰	tán	mucus

No spitting please. *Here's a tissue for you!*

RELATIONSHIPS

34

关系
關係

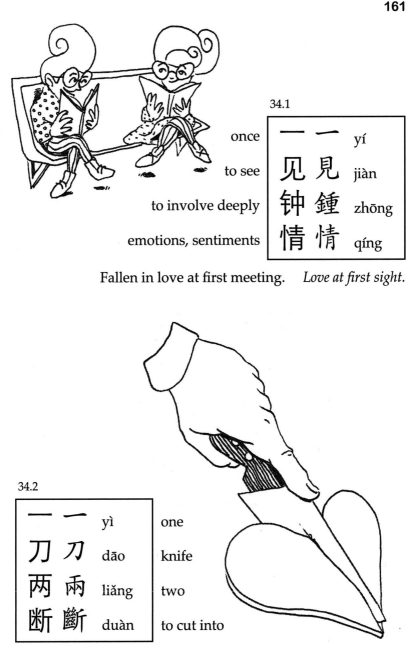

34.1

once	一　一	yí
to see	见　見	jiàn
to involve deeply	钟　鍾	zhōng
emotions, sentiments	情　情	qíng

Fallen in love at first meeting.   *Love at first sight.*

34.2

一　一	yì	one	
刀　刀	dāo	knife	
两　兩	liǎng	two	
断　斷	duàn	to cut into	

Breakup.   Cutting an object into two.

"Dear John....." "You don't bring me flowers anymore." - Lyrics by
Neil Diamond, Alan Bergman and Marilyn Bergman.

Lingering feelings.

34.3

藕	藕	ǒu	lotus root
断	斷	duàn	broken
丝	絲	sī	threads
连	連	lián	to connect

34.4

深	深	shēn	deep
情	情	qíng	feelings
厚	厚	hòu	deep
谊	誼	yì	friendship

True friendship. *Deep as an ocean.*

A very close relationship.

Thick as thieves.

34.5

难	難	nán	difficult
舍	捨	shě	to give up
难	難	nán	difficult
分	分	fēn	to part

34.6

相	相	xiāng	together
依	依	yī	to rely
为	為	wéi	as reason
命	命	mìng	to live

Relying on each other for life.

Inseparable.

TRAFFIC

交通
交通

35.1

四	四	sì	four
通	通	tōng	to go through
八	八	bā	eight
达	達	dá	to reach

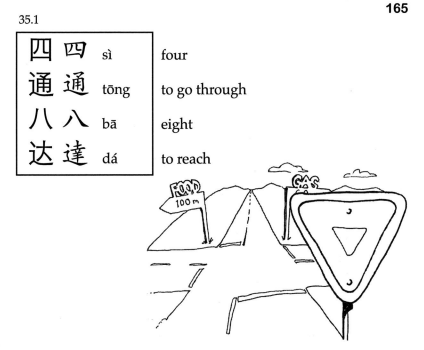

Roads are free and clear in all directions.

No traffic.　　*Any which way you choose.*

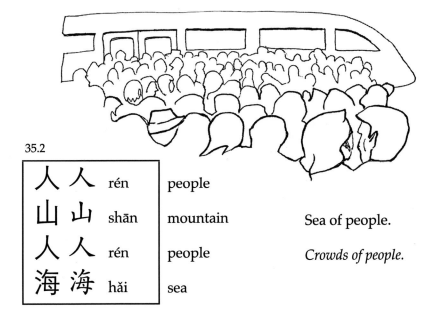

35.2

人	人	rén	people
山	山	shān	mountain
人	人	rén	people
海	海	hǎi	sea

Sea of people.

Crowds of people.

35.3

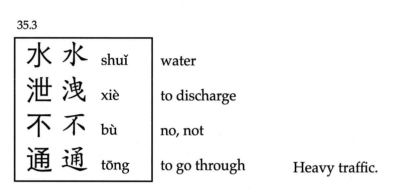

水	水	shuǐ	water
泄	洩	xiè	to discharge
不	不	bù	no, not
通	通	tōng	to go through

Heavy traffic.

Bottleneck. Bumper to bumper.

35.4

不	不	bù	no, not
守	守	shǒu	to keep
秩	秩	zhì	order
序	序	xù	sequence

Disregard of rules and regulations.

Disobeying orders.

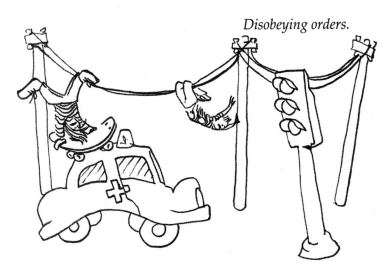

35.5

争	爭	zhēng	to strive
先	先	xiān	forward
恐	恐	kǒng	to be afraid
后	後	hòu	behind

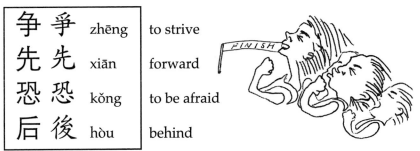

Inching forward to get ahead.

Afraid to lag behind. Rat race.

TRAVEL & LANDMARKS

36

旅游

旅遊

36.1

一	一	yí	one
路	路	lù	trip
平	平	píng	peace
安	安	ān	safe

Wishing you a safe trip!

Safe travels. Bon Voyage!

36.2

古	古	gǔ	old
色	色	sè	scene
古	古	gǔ	old
香	香	xiāng	flavor

Historic sights.

Old world charm.

36.3

Beautiful countryside.	青	青	qīng	green
Pastoral landscape.	山	山	shān	mountains
God's country.	碧	碧	bì	clear
	水	水	shuǐ	waters

36.4

Scenic Vista.	雄	雄	xióng	grandeur
WOW! Breathtaking!	伟	偉	wěi	great
	壮	壯	zhuàng	strong, grand
	观	觀	guān	view

36.5

Sightseeing.	游	遊	yóu	to go sightseeing
The world is your oyster.	山	山	shān	mountains
	玩	玩	wán	to enjoy, to play
	水	水	shuǐ	water

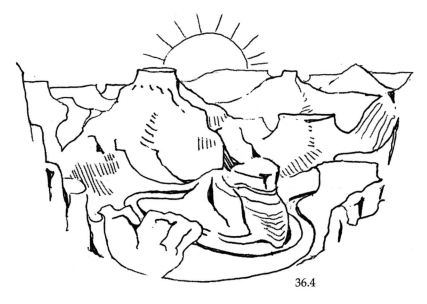

36.3

36.4

36.5

*"There's nothing like Matter
of Fact, Seeing is Believing."*
- J. Arbuthnot Lewis Baboon IV

Once a lively place,
now deserted.

Not a soul in sight!
Ghost town.

36.6

人	人	rén	people
去	去	qù	left
楼	樓	lóu	buildings
空	空	kōng	empty

Homesick.   *Homebound travelers.*

"It's a small world (after all.)" - British songwriters Robert Sherman
and brother Richard Sherman.

36.7

归	歸	guī	to return
心	心	xīn	heart
似	似	sì	like
箭	箭	jiàn	arrow

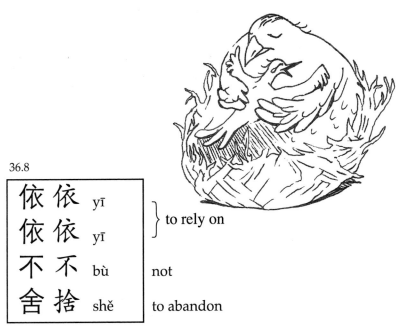

36.8

依	依	yī	} to rely on
依	依	yī	
不	不	bù	not
舍	捨	shě	to abandon

Unwilling to leave a place or person.   Sentimental journey.

"Thanks for the memory." - Lyrics by Leo Robin, later to become a signature tune in Bob Hope's shows.

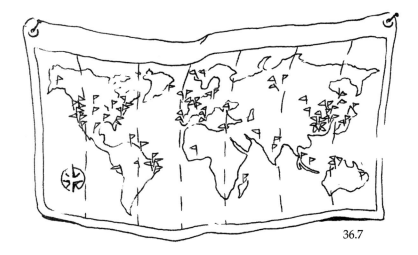

36.7

UNCATEGORIZED

无题

無題

37.1

经	經	jīng	to undergo
久	久	jiǔ	long
耐	耐	nài	to endure
用	用	yòng	to use

Long lasting.

Sturdy. Rock-solid.

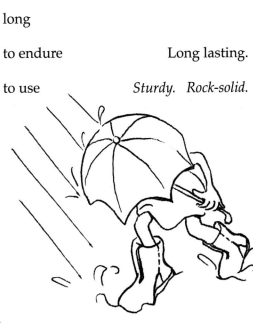

A time of economic and cultural revival.

Renaissance. Boom times.

37.2

黄	黃	huáng	yellow
金	金	jīn	gold
时	時	shí	time
代	代	dài	period

37.3

象	象	xiàng	elephant
牙	牙	yá	ivory tusks
之	之	zhī	of
塔	塔	tǎ	tower

Isolated. An exclusive group of intellectuals disconnected from the everyday world.

Ivory Tower.

37.4

金	金	jīn	gold
玉	玉	yù	jade
良	良	liáng	good
言	言	yán	words

Good Advice. *Words of Wisdom.*

37.5

逼	逼	bī	to force
上	上	shàng	up
梁	梁	liáng	Liang
山	山	shān	Mountain

Under pressure.

Under the gun.

No progress. Falling behind.

One step forward, two steps back.

37.6

不	不	bú	not
进	進	jìn	to advance
则	則	zé	yet
退	退	tuì	to go backward

37.8

37.7

大	大	dà	big
才	才	cái	ability
小	小	xiǎo	little
用	用	yòng	usage

Overqualified.　　*Misjudgement.*

To shoot a mosquito with a cannon.

37.8

火	火	huǒ	fire
上	上	shàng	on
浇	澆	jiāo	to pour
油	油	yóu	oil

←　To make matters worse.　　*Adding insult to injury.*

37.9

答	答	dá	to answer
非	非	fēi	not
所	所	suǒ	that of
问	問	wèn	to ask

Wrong answer.　Not relevant to question.

What does that have to do with the price of tea in China?

WEATHER

38

气候
氣候

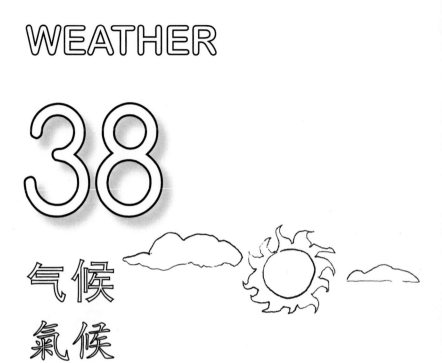

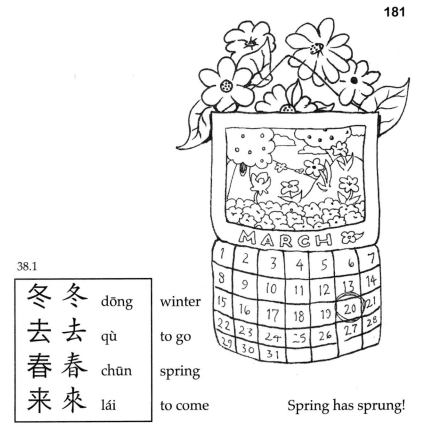

38.1

冬	冬	dōng	winter
去	去	qù	to go
春	春	chūn	spring
来	來	lái	to come

Spring has sprung!

March comes in like a lion and goes out like a lamb. - English proverb

38.2

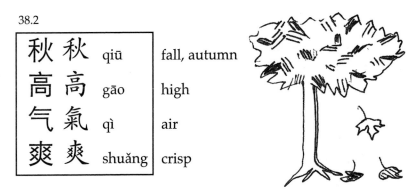

秋	秋	qiū	fall, autumn
高	高	gāo	high
气	氣	qì	air
爽	爽	shuǎng	crisp

Crisp, clear autumn days.

Fall is in the air.

38.3

万	萬	wàn	tens of thousands
里	里	lǐ	miles
无	無	wú	no
云	雲	yún	clouds

Not a cloud in the sky. Blue skies.

"On a clear day, you can see forever."

- Screenplay by Alan Jay Lerner.

38.4

冬	冬	dōng	winter
暖	暖	nuǎn	warm
夏	夏	xià	summer
凉	凉	liáng	cool

Perfect weather.

California here I come!

38.5

狂	狂	kuáng	strong, violent
风	風	fēng	winds
暴	暴	bào	heavy, pounding
雨	雨	yǔ	rain

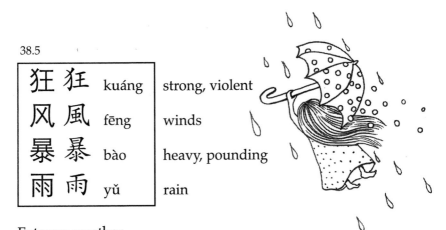

Extreme weather.

A perfect storm.

38.6

天	天	tiān	skies
崩	崩	bēng	to collapse
地	地	dì	earth
裂	裂	liè	to fall apart

Falling skies and earthquake.

FEMA. Seek emergency shelter NOW!

38.7

风	風	fēng	wind
平	平	píng	calm, flat
浪	浪	làng	waves
静	靜	jìng	calm

Calm seas and no wind.

Dead calm.

38.8

电	電	diàn	electricity
闪	閃	shǎn	to flash
雷	雷	léi	thunder
鸣	鳴	míng	to sound

Lightning and thunder.

Seek shelter!

38.9

冰	冰	bīng	ice
天	天	tiān	sky, heaven
雪	雪	xuě	snow
地	地	dì	ground

Arctic blast. Winter wonderland.

"An Old Man's Winter Night" - *Robert Frost*

THE FINALE

39

结局
結局

Chinese New Year's Eve Banquet Menu

年夜飯菜單

Most menus in Chinese restaurants
are in traditional Chinese characters.

COLD PLATTERS	冷盤
Century eggs	松花皮蛋
Jelly fish w/turnip salad	涼拌海蜇
Smoked fish	蜜汁薰魚
Wine drenched chicken	本家醉雞
Five spice beef	五香牛肉
HOT DISHES	熱菜
Shrimp with green peas	青豆炒蝦
Bok choy with shiitake	白菜蘑菇
Lobster Cantonese	港式龍蝦
Steamed perch	清蒸鱸魚
Chicken with salted fish	咸魚雞丁
Stuffed tofu	豆腐扣肉
Roasted Peking Duck	北京烤鴨
Shanghai style noodles	上海炒麵
Braised sea cucumbers	紅燜海參
SOUP	湯
Spare ribs, lotus root	排骨藕湯
DESSERT	點心
Date pancakes	棗泥煎餅

ACKNOWLEDGMENT

I dedicate this book to my family, my sisters Sophia and Lilian, my brother Jim and all our extended families, my friends and students of Chinese language everywhere as well as Chinese-speaking readers learning simple English expressions.

I express my gratitude to Dominic and Kitty Zee, Weicheng Zhong, Mimi Han, Carol Corley, David Li, Jun Wang and Leo Anthony who were the first ones to give support and encouragement.

To Susan Yuan, Matt Casey and Bob Low who simply believed in me, and provided valuable contribution throughout my entire experience, I say "Thank you." Special thanks go to Jing Zhang of Shanghai, China who worked diligently in our final proof-reading.

To all the artists, for their creative work, I congratulate their success in interpreting the idioms and expressions in a most thoughtful and artistic approach. I give them my utmost and sincere wishes in their future endeavor.

Julia Hsu Low
Watertown, Massachusetts
2012

ABOUT THE AUTHOR

Julia Hsu Low / Juliahlow@comcast.net

Julia was born in Shanghai, China in the Year of the Dog. She left China for Taiwan in 1949, and traveled to Hong Kong in 1950 where she attended high school. She completed her college years in Tokyo, Japan and remained there for two more years.

Julia came to New York in 1958 under the MacArthur Refugee Act of 1953. She has lived in Cambridge, Massachusetts for twenty years before settling in Watertown, Massachusetts.

After retirement from Arthur D. Little in 1999. She taught English at a high school in Shanghai, China. In her spare time, Julia has cared for the elderly sick for more than two decades.

CO-EDITOR / TECHNICAL SUPPORT

David Qiang Li / bostonese@gmail.com

David is currently a reporter for the China Press Weekly based in Cambridge, Massachusetts.

David came to Boston in January, 1996 amid a big snow storm. He studied journalism and political science at Suffolk University.

In 1998, he was offered his first job as a reporter with the Singtao Daily Boston Edition, based in Boston's Chinatown. His hobbies include cooking and playing sports.

In March 2012, David founded bostonese.com, an English Chinese Journal online.

CO-EDITOR

Carol Corley / carol.corley@comcast.net

Carol Corley lives with her husband Chris in Newton, Massachusetts. She is a graduate of Boston University.

After a career in financial services, she is spending more time on creative endeavors.

ABOUT THE ARTISTS

Aleks Banner / aleksbanner@gmail.com
Graphic Designer

Aleks currently lives in East Boston, spending his free time gardening and spoiling his two feline flatmates. He holds a B.F.A. from Rhode Island School of Design and is available for freelance work. For inquiries, or to view artwork including drawings, collages, and digital samples please visit his website:

www.aleksbanner.com
or call him 603-897-5472

Erica Femino / eri.femino@gmail.com

Erica Femino is an artist who was born and raised in Boston, MA, where she continues to develop her practice. Erica is a graduate of the Massachusetts College of Art and Design, with a Bachelors of Fine Arts degree in painting. Although she is a painter at heart, Erica also works in many other mediums including illustration, sculpture, video, performance art, installation and poetry. Her website is
www.wix.com/ericafemino/artist

Erica is available for illustration projects, murals, painting commissions, and more. Her phone number is 781-888-8718.